Culinary Arts Institute
BREAD & SOUP
COOKBOOK

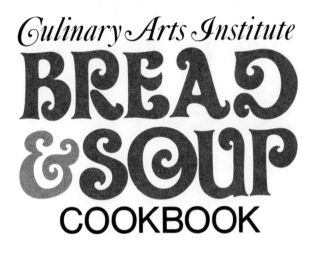

Featured in cover photo:
Mozzarella Egg Bread, 19
Baked Minestrone, 63

BREAD

BREAD AND SOUP COOKBOOK

The Culinary Arts Institute Staff:
Helen Geist: Director
Sherrill Corley: Editor
Edward Finnegan: Executive Editor • Charles Bozett: Art Director
Ethel La Roche: Editorial Assistant • Ivanka Simatic: Recipe Tester
Malinda Miller: Copy Editor • John Mahalek: Art Assembly

Book designed and coordinated by Charles Bozett and Laurel DiGangi

Illustrations by Diana Magnuson

Adventures in Cooking SERIES

& SOUP
COOKBOOK

Culinary Arts Institute

1727 South Indiana Avenue, Chicago, Illinois 60616

Library of Congress Catalog Card Number: 76-26728
International Standard Book Number: 0-8326-0553-0
International Standard Book Number (hard cover): 0-8326-0554-9

PHOTO ACKNOWLEDGMENTS

American Dairy Association; Bob Scott Studios;
Fleischmann's Yeast; The Quaker Oats Company;
United Fresh Fruit and Vegetable Association;
Western Iceberg Lettuce, Inc.; Wheat Flour Institute

FOREWORD

Every hostess enjoys having a specialty all her own to surprise and delight her guests. Making bread and soup may seem like creating magic to some people; however, they are both as easy to make as they are enjoyable to eat. The thrill of taking a few basic ingredients and producing a beautiful loaf of bread or a tantalizing bowl of soup just can't be beat. Together they offer you the greatest chance to be innovative and to add your own personal touches.

The bread section of this book is divided into two parts: yeast breads and quick breads. To show you how easy bread baking is, the step-by-step details of how to combine the ingredients, the part each plays in the development of the dough, and some tips to keep in mind for perfect results are included. To make bread baking satisfying and easy to you, as well as a treat for your friends, there are certain basic principles you need to know. You can refer back to the how-to information as often as needed to clarify or answer questions.

Once you understand the basic principles, you'll find that making bread isn't so hard after all, and that it is worth every minute of the time it takes. Also, the more bread you bake the more adventurous you may find yourself becoming. Looking for new and unusual additions to your favorite recipes may become more than just a casual pastime.

Add a few of the following soup recipes to your list of favorite foods to serve. The variety available is infinite. Soups can be served as light appetizers, additions to a meal, or be robust meals in themselves. Most begin with a basic stock. A soup stock is simply water, meat bones, vegetables, and seasonings that have been simmered to blend the flavors and then strained. Starting from a basic stock, soups can become fancy gourmet dishes or simple down-home meals, all brimming with goodness.

The great thing about soups is that once all the ingredients have been assembled the cook can sit back and let the flavors and aromas slowly simmer to perfection. Be sure to make plenty the first time around so there will be enough for serving later in lunch-box thermoses and other meals.

Included in the book are bread and soup go-togethers and soups for every occasion, from "quick fixings" and lunch-box specials to international favorites. We at CULINARY ARTS INSTITUTE hope this collection will help you discover the exciting world of bread and soup cookery and provide enjoyment for you, your family, and your guests.

CONTENTS

BREAD

There is nothing quite like that delicious aroma of freshly baked bread coming from the kitchen. It says that you have given a part of yourself to your guests or family and that you care. Not only is it appreciated by others, but it gives you a sense of pride in accomplishment. You did it all by yourself!

The first breads were not as luscious as today's version. They were simply whole grain flours mixed with water and baked, resulting in a hard, flat loaf. Later, the Egyptians accidentally discovered that when wild, airborne yeast mixed with the flour-water mixture, it made the dough rise to produce a lighter, larger loaf of bread. Now, yeast has been perfected to give greater control for obtaining beautiful yeast breads every time.

Regardless of your time and schedule, you can choose methods of baking which will allow you the pleasure of having homemade bread whenever you wish.

There are two main categories of bread; those made with yeast and those made without yeast, called quick breads. Today you can make yeast breads in a leisurely way just as your grandmothers did, or in a jiffy to fit your busy schedule.

Whichever method you use, homemade breads will add a special personal touch to any meal.

INGREDIENTS

Each ingredient in bread plays a special part in producing a great-looking and great-tasting loaf.

Knowing and fully understanding the basic steps and terms makes it easy to have perfect results every time.

FLOUR

The "no sift" method of measuring saves lots of time. The milling process sifts the flour, so all you need to do is spoon the flour into a dry measuring cup. Do not scoop or tap the cup. Level it off with a knife or spatula.

The type and quality of flour used in bread baking will determine the final product. Most breads use some portion of wheat flour because it contains a protein called gluten. When the flour is mixed with a liquid and kneaded, it develops an elastic framework which holds the gas bubbles produced by the yeast. This is actually the basic structure of a loaf of bread.

Different flours contain different amounts of gluten. The type of wheat, where it is grown, and the milling process all determine the gluten content. Flours with the highest gluten content will produce the highest loaves.

All-purpose flour is a blend of wheat grains designed to meet general baking needs. It is enriched with the iron and the B vitamins which were lost during the milling process. Chemical agents are added to bleach the flour white and to improve handling and baking properties.

When not stated otherwise, most recipes will mean this type of flour.

Whole wheat flour contains the whole wheat kernel including the bran, endosperm, and germ. Because the germ contains more oil than the rest of the kernel, it has a shorter shelf life than white flour. The tiny rough particles of the bran will cut through the gluten structure and produce a heavier, more compact loaf. Whole wheat flour has a nutty flavor.

Unbleached flour is wheat flour that has had the bran and germ removed and has no preservatives or chemicals added during the milling process. It usually has a higher gluten content, which yields higher loaves.

Rye flour, like whole wheat, will produce a more compact, heavier loaf. Rye breads are usually made with a blend of wheat flour plus rye flour.

Rice flour, rolled oats, soy flour, buckwheat flour are all additions which add a different flavor and texture to a basic bread recipe.

YEAST

Yeast is to be treated with respect because it is a living, microscopic plant. Yeast grows on the sugar in the dough to produce carbon dioxide, which makes the doughs and batters rise. These bubbles of gas are trapped in the gluten structure of the dough and make a light loaf. Yeast can be purchased in two forms and used interchangeably in most recipes.

Active dry yeast looks like tiny, dry granules. It has a life span of several months if kept in a cool, dry place.

Compressed or fresh yeast comes foil- or paper-wrapped in cakes. It is perishable and must be kept in the refrigerator. It may also be frozen. Once defrosted, it must be brought to room

temperature and used right away. Refrigerated, it will keep about two weeks; if frozen, several months.

LIQUIDS

Milk, water, potato water, and fruit juices are the usual liquids called for in bread and roll recipes.

Milk gives bread a velvety, light, smooth crumb and helps keep the bread moist. It also adds important nutrients. Scalding the milk was once necessary to destroy the enzymes which would interfere with the action of the yeast. Since most milk is now pasteurized, this step is no longer necessary. Reconstituted nonfat dry milk and evaporated milk may be substituted.

Water will produce a crisp crust and moist interior. Potato water imparts its own characteristic flavor and texture due to the potato starch it contains.

Fruit juice will give a nice flavor and sweetness to the bread.

SWEETENERS

Sugars are the food yeast cells use to multiply and produce the gas bubbles which cause bread to rise. They contribute a tender crumb, brown crust, and sweet flavor. In small amounts, sugar hastens the yeast's work, but too much inhibits its growth. Most recipes call for granulated sugar, though other sweeteners may be used. However, if you substitute honey, molasses, corn syrup, or maple syrup, you must reduce the amount of liquid accordingly. The dough may be a little stickier to handle and will absorb more flour. These liquid sweeteners will also produce a moister loaf.

FATS

Butter, margarine, shortening, lard, and cooking oils should all be at room temperature before using. They help the dough stretch more easily and produce a richer, more tender, flavorful loaf, as well as giving a soft crust and crumb.

SALT

Salt adds flavor and controls the action of the yeast, thus slowing the rising of the bread.

EGGS

Eggs impart a beautiful color, make the crust tender, and produce a fine-textured crumb. They make a richer and more nutritious loaf. Different-size eggs will affect the amount of liquid in the recipe and perhaps alter the amount of flour needed during the kneading process.

BASIC MIXING METHODS

There are three basic methods for mixing the ingredients for breads. Each one has its advantages and will give you excellent results. Choose one according to your time schedule or preferences. The conventional method produces the old-fashioned, firm-textured loaf. The quick mix method takes the guesswork out of bread baking and is easy to prepare. The batter method uses one-bowl mixing of the batter which is too soft to be kneaded.

CONVENTIONAL OR STRAIGHT DOUGH METHOD

You will probably recognize this method as the one most often used in older recipes. The yeast is dissolved in warm water (105° to 115°) in a large bowl. The warm milk, fat, and salt are stirred into the yeast mixture. Half the flour is added and beaten for a while, and gradually the remaining flour is added.

The temperature of the liquid in which the yeast is dissolved is very important. If the liquid is too hot, it will "kill" the yeast. If it is too cool, it will slow down the action of the yeast. A thermometer is the best guide, but if you don't have one, testing a drop or two on the inside of the wrist will give you a good indication. It is like testing a baby's bottle—if the liquid is a comfortable temperature on the wrist, then it is all right to use.

Sponge method is a variation of the straight dough method. The yeast, sugar, part of the flour, and the liquid are combined and allowed to ferment until the dough is bubbly and "spongelike"—about 15 minutes. Then the remaining ingredients are added. This technique shortens the rising time and gives a more open texture, as you will see in Hurry-Up Dinner Rolls (page 31).

QUICK MIX METHOD

This is the easiest and currently the most popular method of preparing yeast breads. The undissolved dry yeast is mixed with some of the flour, which protects it when the equal amount of hot liquid is added. The hot water may be right from the tap (120° to 130°F), thus eliminating the traditional precision temperature control. Since most recipes call for two packages of yeast and there is no need to dissolve it first, time is saved. The dough also starts out at a warmer temperature perfect for yeast fermentation because of the higher temperature for the liquids. Depending on the amount of flour and sugar, this usually means a shorter rising time. The electric mixer beats the dough for 3 minutes, or it is beaten vigorously by hand for 300 strokes to develop the gluten, so the kneading time is shorter.

BATTER METHOD

There is a larger proportion of liquid to dry ingredients, and no kneading is required. The batter is stirred to develop the gluten and allowed to rise right in the mixing bowl or put into a greased baking pan and then baked. The texture is more open and coarser than a kneaded bread.

TIME-SAVING METHODS

REFRIGERATOR METHOD

The dough is mixed, kneaded, and shaped all at once and then refrigerated for 2 to 24 hours and baked when convenient. The recipes are specially adapted to this way of preparation and sometimes contain a larger portion of sugar for the yeast to feed on. The first fermentation is a short 20-minute rest period and the second is in the refrigerator. Whenever you are ready to bake, allow 10 minutes for the dough to warm up to room temperature.

FREEZER METHOD

The advantage of using a freezer dough recipe is that all the work is done ahead. You can have that aroma of homemade bread baking in a few hours if you have a loaf in the freezer. The dough is mixed, kneaded, and shaped; then frozen without letting it rise. When it is frozen, wrap in moisture-proof wrapping. When ready to use, let it rise until double in bulk (about 4 hours). Bake as usual. The frozen dough will keep 1 to 2 weeks. Large quantities can be made to save time later. Freezer Oatmeal Bread (page 17) is a sure bet.

BROWN AND SERVE METHOD

This allows you to have freshly baked breads anytime. There are two methods from which to choose. Prepare the dough and shape as usual and either bake at a reduced temperature of 250°F for the required time to cook without browning, or bake at the same temperature as the recipe suggests until the bread is almost done but is not browned. Then cool, package, and refrigerate up to one week. When ready to serve, brown in the oven. The loaves may also be frozen about 2 months. Brown-and-Serve Rolls (page 29) is a good example.

SOURDOUGH

Sourdough is in a category all by itself. Its breads have both a unique method of preparation and a delightfully distinctive flavor.

Sourdough breads are made with a "starter" batter which is a mixture of flour, water, and yeast that is allowed to ferment and sour. This "starter" is what leavens the bread and gives it that unusual flavor. There are commercial sourdough starters which you may purchase, or you may "start" your own. By saving some of the fermented brew it is possible to start another batch of sourdough over and over again.

To try your hand at this age-old practice, turn to the recipes for the sourdough starter and breads in the yeast bread section.

BASIC STEPS

Being familiar with the terminology of the art of baking with yeast takes the guesswork out of bread baking and makes it more enjoyable.

KNEADING

Kneading is the fun part of making bread. To actually see and feel that sticky dough change into a silky, smooth elastic ball is really exciting. It is like performing magic right in your kitchen.

Kneading is simply the act of pushing and pulling which develops, smooths, and elasticizes the gluten in the dough. It makes the dough flexible enough to hold the gas bubbles formed by the yeast and forms the bread's structure.

—Lightly dust your hands and a flat surface with flour. Form the dough into a ball and flatten slightly.

—Using the heels of the hands, push the dough away from you. Press as you push. **(A)**

—Turn the dough a quarter of a turn. Fold in half. Repeat the same folding and pushing motion until the dough is smooth and elastic. Dust the surface with flour as needed to prevent stickiness. **(B)**

The dough should be smooth and springy and bounce back when fingers are pushed into the side. The amount of kneading time depends on the gluten in the flour, the type of flour, and the

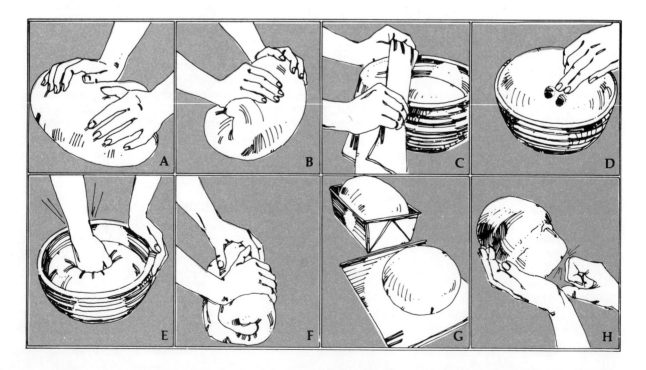

mixing method, but is usually about 5 to 10 minutes.

RISING (proofing)

Yeast needs a warm environment for optimum growth. A draft-free place at a temperature of 80° to 85°F is best. In the conventional method, the dough is placed in a greased bowl and turned once to grease the top, covered lightly, and allowed to rise until double in bulk. This usually takes about 1 hour. The best places for maintaining a warm environment are inside a cupboard, in an unlit oven with a pan of hot water under the dough, or near a radiator. In the quick mix method, the dough "rests" for 20 minutes until puffy. **(C)**

TESTING FOR "DOUBLE IN BULK"

Your eye is a good judge here. If the dough appears to be twice its original size, then it is ready for the next step. The standard test is to lightly press two fingers about 1 inch into the dough. If the dent remains, the dough is double. Doughs will rise faster at high altitudes. If the dough over-rises or even falls, the result will simply be a drier, coarser crumb. **(D)**

PUNCHING DOWN

This is when you can leave your inhibitions behind you. Make a fist and really punch that billowy dough right in the center. This releases the gas, and you are then ready to shape the dough. **(E)**

SHAPING

For rolls and unusual shapes, follow the directions for the individual recipes. To shape loaves:

—Roll dough into a rectangle with a rolling pin or stretch with your hands. This helps release some of the gas bubbles.

—Beginning with the narrow end, roll up tightly, jelly-roll fashion, pressing dough into roll. Pinch the lengthwise seam and tuck under the ends. Place in pans to rise. **(F)**

—Dough may also be shaped in round loaves and placed on greased baking sheets to rise.

SELECTING PANS

The pan size will make a difference. Always follow the recipe suggestions. If the pan is too small, the dough will overflow and be misshapen. If the pan is too large, the loaf will not be high. Most recipes are tested for dull metal pans. Shiny metal pans will take longer to bake the bread. Glass pans need the temperature reduced by 25°F.

BRUSHING CRUST

After the loaves have proofed or risen, you may wish to treat the crusts to make them shiny, crispy, brown, or soft. **(G)**

For a shiny crust, brush the dough with a mixture of egg or egg white and a tablespoon of water before baking. Brushing with egg yolk or milk will give a browner crust. For a crisp, hard crust, brush with water, salt water, or cornstarch and water before and during the baking. For a soft crust, brush with butter before or after the baking.

TELLING WHEN LOAF IS DONE

The eye is a good judge to tell when the bread is finished baking. The loaf should be a light golden brown in color and be slightly shrunken away from the sides of the pan. If you're still not sure, remove the loaf from the pan and thump it on the bottom with your finger. If it sounds hollow, it is done. If not, replace in the pan and return it to the oven for a few minutes longer. **(H)**

FREEZING AND THAWING BREAD

Homemade breads keep best wrapped tightly in plastic wrap or bags or aluminum foil in a cool, dry place. The refrigerator is not the best storage place for bread. Although it helps retard mold growth, it also causes the bread to grow stale more quickly.

To freeze baked breads, completely cool bread or rolls. Wrap tightly in moisture-proof material such as aluminum foil or freezer paper or heavy-duty plastic wrap. Press all the air from the package. Label it with name and date for easy identification. Do not decorate sweet breads before freezing. Breads will stay fresh for 3 to 6 months, depending on the bread and the temperature of the freezer.

To thaw, leave in the original wrapper at room temperature about 2 to 3 hours. Foil-wrapped bread may be reheated in a 350°F oven 20 minutes; then remove the wrapping and continue baking 5 more minutes. Frozen bread slices may be toasted immediately or separated to thaw more quickly, if you are in a hurry.

To freeze unbaked dough, prepare dough and shape as usual. Place in pan without letting it rise. Freeze until firm. Remove from the pan and wrap in aluminum foil or moisture-proof wrapping or bags.

To thaw unbaked dough, replace frozen dough in pan. Brush with oil and let thaw in refrigerator overnight. Remove it to a warm place (80° to 85°F) and let rise until double in bulk. Bake as usual.

YEAST BREAD RECIPES

Now, making the classic white bread can fit into everyone's schedule. Included in the Basic White Bread recipe are two methods of preparation; both make the same great-tasting bread. The Quick Mix Method mixes the yeast with the flour to protect it from the hot liquids. It gives you hot, tasty bread in about two hours. If you choose to make bread the conventional way, first dissolving the yeast in the liquid, you may do other things while the bread is rising.

Basic White Bread

5½ to 6 cups flour
2 packages active dry yeast
2 tablespoons sugar
2 teaspoons salt
1 cup milk
1 cup water
2 tablespoons oil
Oil or butter

QUICK MIX METHOD

1. Combine 2 cups flour, yeast, sugar, and salt in a large mixing bowl.
2. Heat milk, water, and 2 tablespoons oil in a saucepan over low heat until very warm (120° to 130°F).
3. Add liquid to flour mixture; beat on high speed of electric mixer until smooth, about 3 minutes. Gradually stir in more flour to make a soft dough.
4. Turn onto lightly floured surface and knead until smooth and elastic (5 to 10 minutes).
5. Cover dough with bowl or pan; let rest 20 minutes.
6. For two loaves, divide dough in half and roll out two 14×7-inch rectangles; for one loaf roll out to 16×8-inch rectangle.
7. Roll up from narrow side, pressing dough into roll at each turn. Press ends to seal and fold under loaf.
8. Place in 2 greased 8×4×2-inch loaf pans or 1 greased 9×5×3-inch loaf pan; brush with oil.
9. Let rise in warm place until double in bulk (30 to 45 minutes).
10. Bake at 400°F 35 to 40 minutes.
11. Remove from pans immediately and brush with oil; cool on wire rack.

*One 2-pound loaf
or two 1-pound loaves*

CONVENTIONAL METHOD

1. Heat milk, sugar, oil, and salt; cool to lukewarm.
2. In a large bowl, sprinkle yeast in warm water (105° to 115°F); stir until dissolved.
3. Add lukewarm milk mixture and 2 cups flour; beat until smooth.
4. Beat in enough additional flour to make a stiff dough.
5. Turn out onto lightly floured surface; let rest 10 to 15 minutes. Knead until smooth and elastic (8 to 10 minutes).
6. Place in a greased bowl, turning to grease top. Cover; let rise in warm place until double in bulk (about 1 hour).
7. Punch down. Let rest 15 minutes.
8. Follow same shaping and baking instructions as Quick Mix Method.

You'll want to try these flavor variations to the Basic White Bread for something different. Shaping variations are also included.

Cheese Bread: Add **1 cup (4 ounces) shredded Cheddar cheese** before the last portion of the flour.

Onion Bread: Omit the salt and add **1 package (1⅜ ounces) dry onion soup mix** to the warm milk.

Mini Loaves: Divide dough into 10 equal pieces. Shape into loaves. Place in 10 greased 4½×2½×1½-inch loaf pans. Cover; let rise until double in bulk (about 20 minutes). Bake at 350°F 20 to 25 minutes.

Braided Egg Bread: Reduce milk to ½ cup. Add **2 eggs** with warm liquid to the flour mixture. Divide dough into 3 equal pieces. Form each into a rope, 15×12 inches. Braid. Tuck ends under. Place on a greased baking sheet or 9×5×3-inch loaf pan. Cover and let rise and bake the same as basic recipe.

French Bread: Omit the milk and oil and use **2 cups water.** Divide dough in half. Roll each half into 15×12-inch rectangle. Beginning at long side, roll up tightly. Seal seams. Taper the ends. With a sharp knife, make ¼-inch deep diagonal cuts along loaf tops. Cover. Let rise until less than double in bulk (about 20 minutes). Brush with water. Bake at 400°F 15 minutes, then reduce to 350°F and bake 15 to 20 minutes longer. For crisper crust, put pan of hot water in bottom of oven and 5 minutes before loaf is done, brush with glaze of **1 beaten egg white** and **1 tablespoon cold water.**

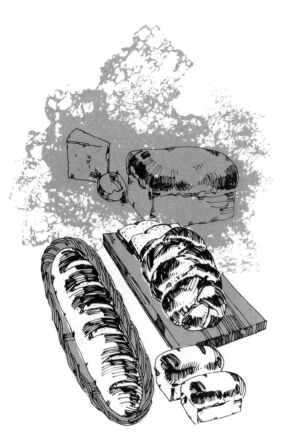

Flavorful Herb Bread

The delicious aroma of the herbs baking in this bread will draw everyone into the kitchen. Be prepared.

¾ **cup warm milk**
2 **tablespoons melted bacon fat or butter**
2 **tablespoons sugar**
1½ **teaspoons salt**
1 **package active dry yeast**
¼ **cup warm water (105° to 115°F)**
1 **egg**
¼ **cup chopped chives**
2 **tablespoons minced parsley**
1 **teaspoon crushed oregano**
3 **to 3½ cups all-purpose flour**

1. Heat milk, bacon fat, sugar, and salt; cool to lukewarm.
2. Sprinkle yeast over warm water in a large mixing bowl; stir until dissolved.
3. Add the liquid, egg, chives, parsley, and oregano to yeast. Stir in 2 cups flour, beating until smooth. Add enough more flour to make a stiff dough.
4. Turn dough onto floured surface; knead until smooth and elastic (10 minutes).
5. Place in a greased bowl, turning to grease top of dough. Cover; let rise in a warm place until double in bulk (1 to 1½ hours).
6. Punch dough down. Shape into a round loaf. Place in a greased 9-inch pie pan. Cover; let rise until double in bulk (about 30 minutes).
7. Bake at 400°F 10 minutes; reduce to 375°F and bake 20 to 25 minutes longer, or until bread is well browned.

1 loaf

100% Whole Wheat Bread

Whole wheat flour gives a sweet, nutty flavor to this bread and is great for toasting. Remember the loaf will be low and compact because of the bran particles cutting through the gluten structure.

4¼ to 4¾ cups whole wheat flour
2 packages active dry yeast
1 tablespoon salt
¾ cup milk
¾ cup water
2 tablespoons oil
2 tablespoons honey
1 egg (at room temperature)
  Oil

1. Combine 1¾ cups flour, yeast, and salt in a large mixing bowl.
2. Heat milk, water, oil, and honey over low heat until very warm (120° to 130°F).
3. Add the liquid and egg to flour mixture; beat until smooth, about 3 minutes on high speed of electric mixer.
4. Gradually stir in more flour to make a soft dough.
5. Turn onto a lightly floured surface and knead until smooth and elastic (5 to 8 minutes).
6. Cover dough with bowl or pan; let rest 20 minutes.
7. Roll out to 16×8-inch rectangle.
8. Roll up from narrow side, pressing dough into roll at each turn. Press ends to seal and fold under loaf.
9. Place in greased 9×5×3-inch loaf pan; brush with oil.
10. Let rise in a warm place (80° to 85°F) until double in bulk (30 to 45 minutes).
11. Bake at 375°F 35 to 40 minutes.
12. Remove from pans immediately and brush with oil or butter; cool on wire rack.

1 loaf

Whole Wheat-Oatmeal Bread

2¼ cups milk
¼ cup butter or margarine
1 tablespoon salt
¼ cup firmly packed brown sugar
2½ to 2¾ cups all-purpose flour
2 cups whole wheat flour
2 packages active dry yeast
2 cups uncooked oats
⅔ cup wheat germ

1. Heat milk, butter, salt, and sugar in a saucepan until lukewarm. Pour liquid into a large mixer bowl. Add 1 cup all-purpose flour and 1 cup whole wheat flour; beat 2 minutes at medium speed of electric mixer. Add remaining whole wheat flour and yeast; beat 2 minutes at medium speed. Stir in oats, wheat germ, and enough additional all-purpose flour to make a soft dough.
2. Turn dough onto a floured surface; knead until smooth and elastic (about 10 minutes). Round dough into a ball. Place in a greased bowl; lightly grease surface of dough. Cover; let rise in a warm place until nearly double in bulk (about 1 hour).
3. Punch dough down; shape into 2 large or 8 miniature loaves. Place in greased 8×4×2-inch or 4×3×2-inch loaf pans. Let rise in a warm place until nearly double in bulk.
4. Bake at 375°F 45 minutes for large loaves or 30 minutes for miniature loaves. Remove from pans immediately; cool on wire rack.

2 large loaves or 8 miniature loaves

Basic White Bread, 14

Delicatessen Rye Bread

You'll notice when making rye breads that the dough is stickier and has a different consistency than whole wheat flour doughs.

2 to 2¾ cups all-purpose or
 unbleached flour
2 cups rye flour
2 teaspoons salt
2 packages active dry yeast
1 tablespoon caraway seed
1 cup milk
¾ cup water
2 tablespoons molasses
2 tablespoons oil

1. Combine 1¾ cups all-purpose flour, salt, yeast, and caraway seed in a large mixing bowl.
2. Heat milk, water, molasses, and oil in a saucepan over low heat until very warm (120° to 130°F).
3. Add liquid gradually to flour mixture, beating on high speed of electric mixer; scrape bowl occasionally. Add 1 cup rye flour, or enough to make a thick batter. Beat at high speed 2 minutes. Stir in remaining rye flour and enough all-purpose flour to make a soft dough.
4. Turn dough onto a floured surface; knead until smooth and elastic (about 5 minutes).
5. Cover with bowl or pan and let rest 20 minutes.
6. Divide in half. Shape into 2 round loaves; place on greased baking sheets. Cover; let rise until double in bulk (30 to 45 minutes).
7. Bake at 375°F 35 to 40 minutes, or until done.

2 loaves

Freezer Oatmeal Bread

This recipe lets you make your own convenience foods. Allow 4 hours after you pull the loaf out of the freezer before you enjoy hot homemade bread.

12 to 13 cups all-purpose flour
 4 packages active dry yeast
 2 tablespoons salt
 2 cups milk
 2 cups water
 ½ cup honey
 ¼ cup vegetable oil
 2 cups uncooked oats
 ½ cup wheat germ
  Oil

1. Combine 2 cups flour, yeast, and salt in a large mixing bowl.
2. Heat milk, water, honey, and oil in a saucepan until very warm (120° to 130°F).
3. Add the liquid gradually to flour mixture, beating 3 minutes on high speed of electric mixer until smooth. Stir in oats, wheat germ, and enough remaining flour to make a soft dough.
4. Turn dough onto a floured surface; knead until smooth and elastic (8 to 10 minutes).
5. Divide dough in quarters. Shape each quarter into a loaf, and either place in an 8×4×2-inch loaf pan or on a baking sheet. Freeze just until firm. Remove from pan. Wrap tightly in aluminum foil or freezer wrap. Dough will keep up to 2 weeks.
6. To bake, remove wrapping and place dough in a greased 8×4×2-inch loaf pan. Thaw in refrigerator overnight or at room temperature 2 hours. Brush with oil and let rise in a warm place until double in bulk (about 2 hours).
7. Bake at 400°F 30 to 35 minutes, or until done.

4 loaves

Freezer Whole Wheat Bread: Follow recipe for Freezer Oatmeal Bread, substituting **5 cups whole wheat flour** for 5 cups all-purpose flour.

Freezer White Bread: Follow recipe for Freezer Oatmeal Bread, omitting oats and wheat germ and increasing flour by about 1 cup.

Russian Kulich, 36;
Kugelhupf, 37;
Austrian Almond Braid, 35

Family Wheat Bread

*This recipe is ideal for your family's everyday bread. It not only makes wonderful sandwiches and toast, .
but is high in protein due to the milk, eggs, and whole grains.*

**5 to 6 cups all-purpose or
    unbleached flour
2 packages active dry yeast
1 tablespoon salt
2 cups milk
½ cup water
¼ cup oil
3 tablespoons honey
3 eggs
2 cups whole wheat flour**

1. Combine 2½ cups all-purpose flour, yeast, and salt in a large mixing bowl.
2. Heat milk, water, oil, and honey in a saucepan until very warm (120° to 130°F).
3. Add liquid to flour mixture and beat until smooth. Add eggs and continue beating about 3 minutes on high speed of electric mixer.
4. Stir in whole wheat flour and enough all-purpose flour to make a soft dough.
5. Turn dough onto a floured surface; allow to rest 10 minutes for easier handling. Knead until smooth and elastic (about 8 minutes). Let rest 20 minutes.
6. Divide dough in half. Roll each half into a 14×9-inch rectangle. Shape into loaves. Place in greased 9×5×3-inch loaf pans.
7. Cover with plastic wrap. Refrigerate 2 to 24 hours.
8. When ready to bake, remove from refrigerator. Let stand at room temperature 10 minutes.
9. Bake at 400°F 40 minutes, or until done.

2 loaves

Variations: Substitute 1 cup of any one of the following ingredients for 1 cup of the whole wheat flour: **uncooked oats, cornmeal, cracked wheat, soybean grits, millet, wheat germ, ground sunflower seeds, bran, crushed shredded wheat cereal,** or any flour of your choice.

Refrigerator Rye Bread

*This lets you do all the mixing and clean up when you have the time and just shape and bake the loaf when
you want to serve hot bread.*

**3 to 3½ cups unbleached or
    all-purpose flour
¼ cup firmly packed brown sugar
2 packages active dry yeast
1 tablespoon salt
1 tablespoon caraway seed or
    grated orange peel
2 cups hot water
¼ cup molasses
2 tablespoons softened butter or
    margarine
3 cups rye flour
    Cornmeal**

1. Combine 2 cups unbleached flour, brown sugar, yeast, salt, and caraway seed in a large mixing bowl.
2. Heat water, molasses, and butter until very warm (120° to 130°F).
3. Add liquid gradually to flour mixture and beat about 3 minutes on high speed of electric mixer. Stir in rye flour and enough unbleached flour to make a soft dough.
4. Turn dough onto a floured surface; knead until smooth and elastic (about 5 minutes). Let rest 20 minutes.
5. Divide dough in half. Shape into 2 long narrow loaves by rolling and stretching dough as for French Bread (page 15). Place on a greased baking sheet sprinkled with cornmeal. Cover with plastic wrap or waxed paper; refrigerate 2 to 24 hours.
6. When ready to bake, remove plastic wrap carefully. Let rise in a warm place while oven is preheating, about 15 minutes. Brush loaves with water.
7. Bake at 400°F 40 minutes, or until done.

2 loaves

Carrot Brown Bread

The husky character of this bread makes it a good companion to soups and a tasty way to get vitamin A.

3 cups whole wheat flour
4 cups unbleached or all-purpose flour
2 packages active dry yeast
2 teaspoons salt
2 cups milk
½ cup water
¼ cup vegetable oil
2 tablespoons honey
2 tablespoons molasses
1 cup grated carrot

1. Mix flours.
2. Combine 2 cups flour mixture, yeast, and salt in a large mixing bowl.
3. Heat milk, water, oil, honey, and molasses in a saucepan until very warm (120° to 130°F).
4. Add liquid gradually to flour mixture, beating 3 minutes on high speed of electric mixer.
5. Stir in carrot and enough more flour to make a soft dough.
6. Turn dough onto a floured surface; allow to rest 10 minutes for easier handling. Knead until smooth and elastic (5 to 8 minutes).
7. Place dough in an oiled bowl; turn to oil top of dough. Cover; let rise in a warm place until double in bulk (about 1 hour).
8. Punch dough down; divide in half. Either shape into 2 round loaves and place on a greased baking sheet, or shape into 2 loaves and place in 2 greased 9×5×3-inch loaf pans. Cover; let rise until double in bulk (about 30 minutes).
9. Bake at 375°F 40 to 45 minutes, or until done.

2 loaves

Mozzarella Egg Bread

7 to 8 cups all-purpose flour
2 packages active dry yeast
1 tablespoon sugar
1 tablespoon salt
6 eggs (at room temperature)
1 cup plain yogurt
2 cups shredded mozzarella cheese (8 ounces)
½ cup hot tap water (120° to 130°F)

1. Combine 2 cups flour, yeast, sugar, and salt in a mixing bowl.
2. Stir eggs, yogurt, 1½ cups cheese, and water into flour mixture; beat until smooth, about 3 minutes on high speed of electric mixer.
3. Stir in enough more flour to make a soft dough.
4. Turn dough onto a floured surface; knead until smooth and elastic (5 to 8 minutes).
5. Place in an oiled bowl; turn to oil top of dough. Cover; let rise in a warm place until double in bulk (about 1 hour).
6. Punch dough down. Divide in half; shape into loaves, and place in 2 greased 9×5×3-inch loaf pans. Cover; let rise until double, about 30 minutes. Top loaves with remaining cheese.
7. Bake at 375°F 30 minutes, or until done.

2 loaves

Hearty Potato Bread

Potato adds wonderful flavor and moistness to bread. Now you have a chance to see why it has been an international favorite for years.

6½ to 7½ cups flour
2 packages active dry yeast
2 tablespoons sugar
1 tablespoon salt
2¼ cups hot potato water
1 cup warm unseasoned mashed
    potatoes
2 tablespoons oil

1. Combine flour, yeast, sugar, and salt in a large mixing bowl.
2. Add potato water (see Note), potatoes, and oil to flour mixture; beat about 3 minutes on high speed of electric mixer.
3. Stir in enough more flour to make a soft dough.
4. Turn dough onto a floured surface; knead until smooth and elastic (5 to 8 minutes).
5. Place in an oiled bowl; turn to oil top of dough. Cover; let rise in a warm place until double in bulk (about 1 hour).
6. Punch dough down. Divide in half; shape into loaves and place in 2 greased 9×5×3-inch loaf pans. Cover; let rise until double in bulk (about 45 minutes).
7. Bake at 375°F 40 to 45 minutes, or until done.

2 loaves

Note: To make potato water, cook 2 pared, cut-up potatoes until tender in about 3 cups water. Drain, reserving water. Mash potatoes and cool for bread.

Colonial Bread

2 cups whole wheat flour
2½ cups unbleached or all-purpose
    flour
¾ cup rye flour
½ cup yellow cornmeal
⅓ cup firmly packed brown sugar
2 packages active dry yeast
1 tablespoon salt
2½ cups hot tap water (120° to
    130°F)
¼ cup vegetable oil
1 egg

1. Blend flours and cornmeal. Combine 2½ cups flour mixture, sugar, yeast, and salt in a large mixing bowl.
2. Stir water, oil, and egg into flour mixture; beat until smooth, about 3 minutes on high speed of electric mixer.
3. Gradually stir in enough more flour mixture to make a soft dough.
4. Turn dough onto a floured surface; knead until smooth and elastic (5 to 8 minutes).
5. Place in an oiled bowl; turn to oil top of dough. Cover; let rise in a warm place until double in bulk (about 1 hour).
6. Punch dough down. Divide in half; shape into loaves. Place in 2 greased 9×5×3-inch loaf pans. Cover; let rise until double in bulk (about 30 minutes).
7. Bake at 375°F 35 to 40 minutes, or until done.

2 loaves

Cornmeal French Bread

1 cup cooked cornmeal mush (see recipe)
2 packages active dry yeast
½ cup warm water
1 cup milk, scalded
1 tablespoon sugar
2½ teaspoons salt
4¾ to 5¼ cups all-purpose flour

1. Prepare cornmeal mush; cool slightly.
2. Dissolve yeast in warm water.
3. Pour scalded milk over sugar and salt in a large bowl. Add mush and mix well; cool to lukewarm. Beat in 1 cup flour. Mix in yeast and enough additional flour to make a soft dough.
4. Turn dough onto a lightly floured surface. Knead until smooth and satiny (about 10 minutes).
5. Put dough into a greased bowl; turn to grease top. Cover; let rise in a warm place until double in bulk (about 1 hour).
6. Punch dough down; cover and let rest 10 minutes. Form into a long thin roll on greased baking sheet. With a sharp knife, cut diagonal ¼-inch-deep slits about 2½ inches apart across the top. Brush top of loaf with salt water (**1 tablespoon salt** dissolved in **¼ cup water).** Cover; let rise until double in bulk (about 45 minutes).
7. Pour boiling water into a pie pan to a ½-inch depth; set on bottom rack of oven.
8. Bake at 400°F 15 minutes; turn temperature control to 350°F and bake 30 to 35 minutes longer. About 5 minutes before bread is finished baking, baste with salt water.

1 large loaf

Cornmeal Mush: Heat **3 cups water** to boiling in a saucepan. Mix **1 cup cornmeal, 1 teaspoon salt,** and **1 cup cold water.** Pour cornmeal mixture into boiling water, stirring constantly. Cook until thickened, stirring frequently. Cover; continue cooking over low heat 10 minutes.

4 cups

Here's-To-Your-Health Bread

Just about every ingredient in this bread is good for you. Whole grains and cottage cheese provide protein. Raisins and molasses contribute important minerals, especially iron. And besides all this, it tastes delicious.

4½ cups all-purpose or unbleached flour
3 cups whole wheat flour
1 cup uncooked oats
½ cup wheat germ
2 packages active dry yeast
2 teaspoons salt
2½ cups hot tap water (120° to 130°F)
1½ cups (12 ounces) creamed cottage cheese (at room temperature)
½ cup molasses or honey
2 tablespoons vegetable oil
1 cup raisins

1. Mix flours and oats.
2. Combine 3 cups flour mixture, wheat germ, yeast, and salt in a large mixing bowl.
3. Add water, cottage cheese, molasses, and oil to flour mixture; beat until smooth, about 3 minutes on high speed of electric mixer.
4. Stir in raisins and enough more flour to make a soft dough.
5. Turn dough onto a floured surface; let rest 10 minutes for easier handling. Knead until smooth and elastic (5 to 8 minutes).
6. Place in an oiled bowl; turn dough to oil top. Cover; let rise in a warm place until double in bulk (about 1 hour).
7. Punch dough down. Divide dough in thirds; shape into loaves and place in 3 greased 9×5×3-inch loaf pans. Cover; let rise until double in bulk (about 30 minutes).
8. Bake at 375°F 30 to 35 minutes, or until done.

3 loaves

Cinnamon Swirl Loaves

2 packages active dry yeast
½ cup warm water
2 cups milk, heated
⅓ cup honey
1 tablespoon salt
⅓ cup shortening
5 to 5½ cups all-purpose flour
2 cups uncooked oats
½ cup firmly packed brown sugar
2 tablespoons cinnamon

1. Dissolve yeast in warm water.
2. Pour hot milk over honey, salt, and shortening in a large bowl. Cool to lukewarm. Stir in 1 cup flour. Add softened yeast and oats. Stir in enough more flour to make a soft dough.
3. Turn dough onto a lightly floured surface; knead until smooth and satiny (about 10 minutes). Round dough into a ball and place in a greased bowl. Brush lightly with melted shortening. Cover; let rise in a warm place until double in bulk (about 1 hour).
4. Punch dough down; divide in half. Roll each half into a 14×7-inch rectangle. Brush with melted butter; sprinkle with brown sugar and cinnamon. Starting with short side, roll up as for jelly roll.
5. Place in 2 greased 8×4×2-inch loaf pans. Brush lightly with **melted shortening.** Cover; let rise until nearly double in bulk (about 45 minutes).
6. Bake at 375°F 45 to 50 minutes. Remove loaves from pans and brush with **melted butter.** Cool. Drizzle with a thin confectioners' sugar glaze, if desired.

2 loaves

Triple Treat Bread

If you don't have dry milk, you can replace 1 cup of the water with milk for the same tasty results.

4½ cups all-purpose or unbleached flour
2 cups whole wheat flour
1 cup rye flour
½ cup firmly packed brown sugar
½ cup instant nonfat dry milk
2 packages active dry yeast
1 tablespoon salt
2 cups hot tap water (120° to 130°F)
¼ cup vegetable oil

1. Mix flour.
2. Combine 2 cups flour mixture, sugar, dry milk, yeast, and salt in a large mixing bowl.
3. Stir water and oil into flour mixture; beat until smooth, about 3 minutes on high speed of electric mixer. Stir in enough remaining flour to make a soft dough.
4. Turn dough onto a floured surface; knead until smooth and elastic (5 to 8 minutes).
5. Place in an oiled bowl; turn to oil top of dough. Cover; let rise in a warm place until double (about 45 minutes).
6. Punch dough down. Divide in half; shape into loaves and place in 2 greased 9×5×3-inch loaf pans. Cover; let rise until double in bulk (about 30 minutes).
7. Bake at 375°F 35 to 40 minutes, or until done.

2 loaves

Ground Nut Bread

The electric blender or food processor is perfect for grinding the nuts and sunflower seeds for this bread.

3 cups all-purpose flour
1½ cups whole wheat flour
2 packages active dry yeast
2 teaspoons salt
1¾ cups hot tap water (120° to 130°F)
¼ cup honey

1. Mix flours.
2. Combine 1¾ cups flour mixture, yeast, and salt in a large mixing bowl.
3. Add water, honey, and oil to flour mixture; beat until smooth, about 3 minutes on high speed of electric mixer.
4. Stir in oats, nuts, sunflower seeds, cornmeal, and enough more flour to make a soft dough.

2 tablespoons vegetable oil
1 cup rolled oats
1 cup ground unsalted nuts
½ cup ground unsalted hulled
    sunflower seeds
½ cup cornmeal

5. Turn dough onto a floured board; knead until smooth and elastic (5 to 8 minutes).
6. Place in an oiled bowl; turn to oil top of dough. Cover; let rise in a warm place until double in bulk (about 1 hour).
7. Punch dough down. Divide in half, then each half in thirds. Form each piece into a rope 12 to 15 inches long. For each loaf, braid 3 pieces together. Tuck ends under; place in 2 greased 9×5×3-inch loaf pans or on greased baking sheets. Cover; let rise until double in bulk (about 1 hour).
8. Bake at 375°F 35 to 40 minutes, or until done.

2 loaves

Harvest Bread

1½ cups milk
⅓ cup margarine
2 tablespoons honey
2 tablespoons light molasses
2 teaspoons salt
2 large shredded wheat biscuits,
    crumbled
½ cup warm water (105° to 115°F)
2 packages active dry yeast
2 cups whole wheat flour
¼ cup wheat germ
2 to 3 cups all-purpose flour

1. Heat milk; stir in margarine, honey, molasses, salt, and shredded wheat biscuits. Cool to lukewarm.
2. Measure warm water into a large warm bowl. Sprinkle in yeast; stir until dissolved. Add lukewarm milk mixture and whole wheat flour; beat until smooth. Stir in wheat germ and enough all-purpose flour to make a stiff dough.
3. Turn dough onto a lightly floured surface; knead until smooth and elastic (8 to 10 minutes). Place in a greased bowl; turn to grease top. Cover; let rise in a warm place until double in bulk (about 1 hour).
4. Punch dough down; divide in half. Proceed, following directions below for desired shape.
5. Cover; let rise in a warm place until double in bulk (about 1 hour). If making sheaf, make diagonal snips with scissors along the bent portion of stalks above the twist. If desired, gently brush sheaf with beaten egg.
6. Bake on lowest rack position at 400°F about 20 minutes for sheaves and 25 to 30 minutes for loaves, or until done. Remove from baking sheets and cool on wire racks.

2 loaves

To Make Round Loaves: Shape each half of dough into a smooth round ball. Press each ball slightly to flatten into rounds 6 inches in diameter. Place on greased baking sheets.

To Make Wheat Sheaf: Divide one half of dough into 18 equal pieces. Roll 2 pieces into 12-inch ropes. Twist ropes together; set aside. Roll 8 pieces into 18-inch ropes and roll remaining 8 pieces into 15-inch ropes. Place one 18-inch rope lengthwise on center of a greased baking sheet, bending top third of rope off to the left at a 45-degree angle. Place a second 18-inch rope on sheet touching the first rope but bending top third off to the right. Repeat procedure using two more 18-inch ropes, placing them along outer edges of straight section and inside bent sections so that ropes are touching. Repeat, using two of the 15-inch ropes. Repeat, starting with the long ropes, placing them on top of the arranged long ropes and slightly spreading out ropes forming bottom of sheaf. Fill in by topping with the remaining 15-inch ropes, making shorter bends in two uppermost ropes. Cut twist in half. Arrange twists side by side around center of sheaf, tuck ends underneath. Repeat with remaining half of dough.

Mushroom Bread

¼ cup margarine
½ pound mushrooms, finely chopped
1 cup finely chopped onion
2 cups milk
3 tablespoons molasses
4 teaspoons salt
¼ teaspoon pepper
½ cup warm water (105° to 115°F)
2 packages active dry yeast
1 egg
1 cup wheat germ
8 to 9 cups all-purpose flour

1. Melt 2 tablespoons margarine in a large skillet over medium heat. Add mushrooms and onion; sauté until onion is tender and liquid has evaporated. Cool.
2. Heat milk; stir in molasses, salt, and pepper. Cool to lukewarm.
3. Measure warm water into a large warm bowl. Sprinkle in yeast; stir until dissolved. Add lukewarm milk mixture, egg, wheat germ, and 2 cups flour; beat until smooth. Stir in enough additional flour to make a stiff dough.
4. Turn dough onto a lightly floured surface; knead until smooth and elastic (8 to 10 minutes). Place in a greased bowl; turn to grease top. Cover; let rise in a warm place until double in bulk (about 1 hour).
5. Meanwhile, use four 30-ounce fruit cans to prepare Mushroom Pans (see below).
6. Punch dough down; turn onto lightly floured surface.

To Make Mushrooms: Divide dough onto 4 equal pieces. Shape each piece into a smooth round ball. Place in prepared Mushroom Pans. Let rise in a warm place until double in bulk (about 1 hour). With fingertips, gently press lower edge of mushroom cap down to meet foil-covered collar. Reshape cap if necessary. If desired, brush mushrooms with a mixture of 1 egg beaten with 1 tablespoon water. Bake on lowest rack position at 400°F about 40 minutes, or until done. Carefully remove from pans and cool on wire racks.

To Make Loaves: Divide dough in half. Roll each half to a 14×9-inch rectangle. Shape into loaves. Place in 2 greased 9×5×3-inch loaf pans. Cover; let rise in a warm place until double in bulk (about 1 hour). Bake at 400°F about 45 minutes, or until done. Remove from pans and cool on wire racks.

*4 mushrooms
or 2 round loaves*

Mushroom Pans: Cut 4 heavy cardboard squares 2 inches wider than can opening. Trace can opening in center of squares and cut out. Cover rings with foil. Place rings over cans so they fit tightly around opening. Grease cans and foil collars well.

Anadama Batter Bread

1 package active dry yeast
¼ cup warm water
1 cup cornmeal
2 teaspoons salt
½ teaspoon baking soda
⅓ cup dark molasses
3 tablespoons shortening
¾ cup boiling water

1. Dissolve yeast in warm water.
2. Combine cornmeal, salt, baking soda, molasses, and shortening in a large mixer bowl. Stir in boiling water; cool to lukewarm.
3. Add softened yeast, egg, and 1 cup flour to cornmeal mixture; beat 2 minutes on medium speed of electric mixer or 300 vigorous strokes with a wooden spoon. Stir in remaining flour.

1 egg
2¼ cups all-purpose flour
Melted butter

4. Spread batter in a well-greased 2-quart casserole. Cover; let rise in a warm place until nearly double in bulk (1 to 1½ hours).
5. Bake at 350°F about 40 minutes. Remove from casserole immediately. Brush top lightly with melted butter; cool.

1 loaf

Aspen Batter Bread

4 cups all-purpose flour
2 tablespoons sugar
1 package active dry yeast
1 teaspoon salt
¼ teaspoon ginger
1 can (13 ounces) evaporated milk
½ cup hot water
2 tablespoons vegetable oil

1. Combine 2 cups flour, sugar, yeast, salt, and ginger in a large mixing bowl.
2. Heat milk, water, and oil until very warm (120° to 130°F).
3. Stir in liquid with flour mixture; beat 2 minutes by hand or with electric mixer. Cover; let rise 15 minutes.
4. Beat in remaining flour by hand. Pour into 2 greased 1-pound coffee cans. Cover with greased plastic lids; let rise in a warm place until dough rises to top of cans (or until lids pop off), about 35 minutes. Remove lids.
5. Bake at 375°F 40 to 45 minutes, or until done. Place on wire racks to cool slightly before removing loaves from cans.

2 loaves

Bran-New Batter Bread

1 cup all-purpose flour
1 package active dry yeast
2 teaspoons salt
½ cup hot water
½ cup milk
½ cup vegetable oil
⅓ cup honey
2 eggs
1 cup whole bran cereal
½ cup wheat germ
1½ cups all-purpose flour

1. Combine 1 cup flour, yeast, and salt in large mixing bowl.
2. Heat water, milk, oil, and honey until very warm (120° to 130°F).
3. Add liquid and eggs to flour mixture and beat about 3 minutes at high speed of electric mixer.
4. Beat in bran cereal, wheat germ, and remaining flour by hand. Divide mixture into 2 well-greased 1-pound coffee cans. Cover with greased plastic lids and let rise in a warm place until dough rises almost to top of cans (about 35 minutes). Remove lids.
5. Bake at 375°F 35 minutes, or until done. Place on wire racks. Cool loaves slightly, then remove from cans and place on racks to cool.

2 loaves

Dilly Cottage Batter Bread

2½ cups all-purpose flour
1 package active dry yeast
1 tablespoon instant minced onion
1 teaspoon salt
½ teaspoon dill weed, thyme, or rosemary
1 cup creamed cottage cheese (at room temperature)
½ cup hot tap water (120° to 130°F)
1 egg (at room temperature)
1 tablespoon honey
1½ cups all-purpose flour

1. Combine 1 cup flour, yeast, onion, salt, and dill weed.
2. Add cottage cheese, water, egg, and honey to flour mixture; beat 3 minutes by hand or with electric mixer.
3. Beat in remaining flour. Cover; let rise in a warm place until double in bulk (about 1 hour).
4. Stir batter down; pour into a well-greased 1½-quart round casserole. Let rise in a warm place until light (30 to 40 minutes).
5. Bake at 375°F 50 to 55 minutes, or until done.

1 loaf

Add variety to your life and to your dinner parties with a myriad of rolls—all of which spring from one basic dough. All of these rolls freeze well after baking, ready to be served after a brief thawing or warming in aluminum foil in the oven. Whether you feature one kind, or an assortment, they will lend distinction to any meal and bring raves from your family and guests. For moist, tender rolls, the dough should be soft. Therefore, you'll want to avoid incorporating too much flour during the kneading.

Basic Dinner Rolls

4 to 4¾ cups all-purpose flour
2 tablespoons sugar
2 packages active dry yeast
1 teaspoon salt
1 cup milk
½ cup water
¼ cup butter or margarine
1 egg (at room temperature)
Melted butter (optional)

1. Combine 1½ cups flour, sugar, yeast, and salt in a mixing bowl.
2. Heat milk, water, and butter until very warm (120° to 130°F).
3. Add liquid and egg to flour mixture; beat until smooth, about 3 minutes.
4. Stir in enough remaining flour to make a soft, sticky dough.
5. Turn dough onto a floured surface; continue to work in flour until dough can be kneaded. Knead until smooth and elastic, but still soft (about 5 minutes).
6. Cover dough with bowl or pan. Let rest 20 minutes.
7. Shape dough as desired. Cover and let rise until double in bulk (about 15 minutes).
8. Bake at 425°F about 12 minutes. Cool on wire racks. Brush with butter if desired.

2 to 2½ dozen rolls

Pan Rolls: Divide dough into 24 equal pieces by first dividing dough in half and then each half into 12 equal pieces. Roll into balls. Place in a greased 13×9×2-inch baking pan. Brush with melted butter, if desired.

Cloverleaf Rolls: Pinch off bits of dough; roll into 1-inch balls. For each roll, place 3 balls in a greased muffin-pan well.

Crescents: Divide dough in half. Roll each half into a 12-inch round about ¼ inch thick. Brush with **2 tablespoons melted butter.** Cut into 12 wedges. For each crescent, roll up wedge beginning at side opposite the point. Place point-side down on a greased baking sheet; curve ends.

Snails: Roll dough into a rectangle ¼ inch thick. Cut off strips ½ inch wide and 5 inches long. Roll each piece of dough into a rope about 10 inches long. Wind into a flat coil, tucking ends under. Place on greased baking sheet.

Figure Eights: Shape strips of dough ½ inch wide and 5 inches long into 10-inch ropes as in Snails (above). For each roll, pinch ends of rope together and twist once to form a figure 8. Place on greased baking sheets.

Twists: Follow procedure for Figure Eights, giving each 8 an additional twist.

Bowknots: Roll dough into a rectangle ¼ inch thick. Cut off strips ½ inch wide and 5 inches long. Roll each strip into a smooth rope 9 or 10 inches long. Gently tie into a single or double knot. Place on a greased baking sheet.

Parker House Rolls: Roll dough ¼ inch thick. Brush with **3 or 4 tablespoons melted butter.** Cut with a 2½-inch round cutter. With a knife handle, make a crease across each circle slightly off center. Fold larger half over the smaller, pressing edges to seal. Place on a greased baking sheet or close together in a greased 13×9×2-inch baking pan.

Braids: Form several ropes, ½ inch in diameter. Braid 3 ropes into a long strip; cut into 3-inch lengths. Pinch together at each end. Place on a greased baking sheet.

Butterflies: Divide dough in half. Roll each half into a 24×6-inch rectangle about ¼ inch thick. Brush with **2 tablespoons melted butter.** Starting with long side, roll up dough as for jelly roll. Cut off 2-inch pieces. With handle of knife, press crosswise at center of each roll, forming a deep groove so spiral sides become visible. Place on a greased baking sheet.

Fantans or Butterflake Rolls: Roll dough into a rectangle ¼ inch thick. Brush with **3 or 4 tablespoons melted butter.** Cut into 1-inch strips. Stack 6 or 7 strips; cut each into 1½-inch sections. Place on end in greased muffin-pan wells.

Crusty Hard Rolls

If you like a crunchy roll, try this one. A shiny golden crust surrounds the snowy white and moist interior.

3½ to 4½ cups all-purpose flour
2 packages active dry yeast
1 tablespoon sugar
1½ teaspoons salt
1 cup hot tap water (120° to 130°F)
2 tablespoons vegetable oil
1 egg white
1 egg yolk
1 tablespoon water

1. Combine 1 cup flour, yeast, sugar, and salt in a large mixer bowl. Stir in water, oil, and egg white; beat until smooth, about 3 minutes on high speed of electric mixer. Gradually stir in more flour to make a soft dough.
2. Turn dough onto a floured surface; knead until smooth and elastic (3 to 5 minutes).
3. Cover with bowl or pan and let rest about 20 minutes.
4. Divide into 18 equal pieces. Form each into a smooth oval; place on a greased baking sheet. Slash tops lengthwise about ¼ inch deep. Let rise until double in bulk (about 15 minutes).
5. Brush with a mixture of egg yolk and 1 tablespoon water.
6. Bake at 400°F 15 to 20 minutes. For a crisper crust, place a shallow pan of hot water on lowest oven rack during baking.

1½ dozen rolls

Kaiser Rolls: Follow recipe for Crusty Hard Rolls, only flatten each of the 18 pieces of dough into 4- to 4-½-inch rounds. For each roll, lift one edge of the round and press it into center of circle. Then lift the corner of the fold and press it into the center. Continue clockwise around the circle until 5 or 6 folds have been made. Let rise and bake as directed above.

French Crescents (Croissants)

Crescents are a lot of work but since they melt in your mouth they're worth every minute.

- 1 cup milk
- 1 tablespoon oil
- 1 tablespoon sugar
- ½ teaspoon salt
- 1 package compressed or active dry yeast
- ¼ cup warm water (105° to 115°F)
- 2¾ to 3 cups all-purpose flour
- 1 cup (½ pound) butter, softened
- 1 egg yolk
- 1 tablespoon milk

1. Heat 1 cup milk, oil, sugar, and salt in a saucepan; cool to lukewarm.
2. Dissolve yeast in warm water in a large bowl. Add milk mixture and 1 cup flour; beat until smooth. Stir in enough remaining flour to make a soft dough.
3. Turn dough onto a floured surface; continue to work in flour until dough can be kneaded. Knead until smooth and elastic (about 5 minutes).
4. Shape dough into a ball and place in an oiled bowl; turn to oil top of dough. Cover; let rise in a warm place until double in bulk (about 45 minutes).
5. Punch dough down. Roll out on floured surface to form a rectangle about ¼ inch thick.
6. Cut butter in slices (just soft enough to spread but not melted). Spread over center one-third section of rectangle. Fold each extending side over butter, pressing together the open edges to seal. Roll out again until rectangle is ⅜ inch thick. Turn dough occasionally, flouring surface lightly to prevent sticking. Fold in thirds again to make a squarish rectangle. Roll dough and fold again in the same manner. Wrap dough in waxed paper or foil; chill 30 minutes. If at any time dough oozes butter and becomes sticky while rolling, chill until butter is more firm.
7. Roll and fold again 2 more times exactly as directed before. Chill dough again another 30 minutes.
8. Roll dough into a rectangle about ⅛ inch thick. Cut into strips 6 inches wide. Cut triangles out of each strip to measure about 6×8×6 inches. Roll up each triangle of dough from a 6-inch edge, pinching tip to seal. Shape each roll into a crescent. Place, point down, 1½ inches apart on ungreased baking sheet.
9. Cover; let rise until double in bulk (30 to 45 minutes).
10. Brush each roll with mixture of egg yolk and 1 tablespoon milk.
11. Bake at 425°F 15 minutes, or until brown. Remove from baking sheet and cool on wire rack. Serve warm.

About 1½ dozen rolls

Pumpkin Spice Rolls

- 3½ to 4½ cups all-purpose flour
- ¼ cup firmly packed brown sugar
- 1 package active dry yeast
- 1 teaspoon salt
- ½ teaspoon cinnamon
- ¼ teaspoon nutmeg
- ⅛ teaspoon cloves
- ⅛ teaspoon ginger
- 1 cup milk
- ¼ cup water

1. Combine 1½ cups flour, brown sugar, yeast, salt, and spices in a large mixer bowl.
2. Heat milk, water, pumpkin, and oil in a saucepan until very warm (120° to 130°F).
3. Add liquid and egg to flour mixture and beat until smooth, about 3 minutes on high speed of electric mixer.
4. Stir in enough remaining flour to make a soft dough.
5. Turn dough onto floured board; continue to work in flour until dough is stiff enough to knead. Knead until smooth and elastic (about 5 minutes).

¾ cup canned pumpkin
¼ cup vegetable oil
1 egg
2 tablespoons melted butter

6. Cover with bowl or pan; let rest 20 minutes.
7. Shape into 2-inch balls; place each ball in a greased muffin-pan well. Brush with melted butter. Cover; let rise until double in bulk (about 20 minutes).
8. Bake at 375°F 20 minutes, or until done.

2 dozen rolls

Potato Pan Rolls

½ cup milk
1 tablespoon sugar
¾ teaspoon salt
2 tablespoons margarine
½ cup warm water (105° to 115°F)
1 package active dry yeast
1 egg
½ cup mashed potatoes (at room temperature)
3½ to 4½ cups all-purpose flour
Flour for dusting

1. Heat milk; stir in sugar, salt, and margarine. Cool to lukewarm.
2. Measure warm water into a large warm bowl. Sprinkle in yeast; stir until dissolved. Stir in lukewarm milk mixture, egg, mashed potatoes, and 2 cups flour. Beat until smooth. Stir in enough additional flour to make a soft dough.
3. Turn dough onto a lightly floured surface; knead until smooth and elastic (8 to 10 minutes). Place in a greased bowl; turn to grease top. Cover; let rise in a warm place until double in bulk (about 1 hour).
4. Punch dough down; turn out onto a lightly floured surface. Divide in half. Divide each half into 16 equal pieces; form into smooth balls. Place in 2 greased 9-inch round layer cake pans. Cover; let rise in a warm place until double in bulk (about 1 hour).
5. Dust rolls with flour.
6. Bake at 375°F about 25 minutes, or until done. Remove from pans and cool on wire racks.

32 rolls

Brown-and-Serve Rolls

9 to 10 cups all-purpose flour
½ cup sugar
2 packages active dry yeast
1 tablespoon salt
2 cups warm water
1 cup milk
½ cup butter or margarine

1. Stir together 3 cups flour, sugar, yeast, and salt in a large mixer bowl.
2. Heat water, milk, and butter until very warm (120° to 130°F).
3. Add liquid ingredients to flour mixture; beat until smooth, about 3 minutes on high speed of electric mixer.
4. Gradually stir in enough more flour to make a soft dough.
5. Turn out onto a floured surface; knead until smooth and elastic (5 to 8 minutes).
6. Shape dough into a ball, place in an oiled bowl, and turn to oil top of dough. Cover; let rise in a warm place until double in bulk (30 to 45 minutes).
7. Punch dough down. Divide in half. Shape each half into rolls (see page 26 for different shapes). Let rise in a warm place until double in bulk (30 to 45 minutes).
8. Bake at 375°F 20 to 25 minutes, or just until rolls begin to change color. Cool in pans 20 minutes. Finish cooling on wire racks. Wrap tightly in plastic bags and refrigerate up to 1 week, or freeze up to 2 months. Before serving, place rolls on ungreased baking sheet.
9. Bake at 400°F 10 to 12 minutes.

About 4 dozen rolls

Better Batter Rolls

These rolls resemble muffins in texture and shape, but the aroma as they bake is unmistakably and deliciously that of yeast. These go together quickly as they require no kneading.

3 cups all-purpose flour
1 package active dry yeast
1 teaspoon salt
1 cup hot water
¼ cup vegetable oil
¼ cup honey
1 egg

1. Combine 2 cups flour, yeast, and salt in a mixer bowl. Add water, oil, honey, and egg; beat until smooth, about 2 minutes on medium speed of electric mixer or 300 vigorous strokes by hand.
2. Beat in remaining flour by hand. Cover; let rise until double in bulk (about 30 minutes).
3. Fill greased muffin-pan wells half full. Let rise until double in bulk (about 30 minutes).
4. Bake at 400°F 10 to 12 minutes.

2 dozen rolls

English Muffins

3 to 3½ cups all-purpose flour
2 tablespoons sugar
1 package active dry yeast
1 teaspoon salt
¾ cup hot milk (120° to 130°F)
1 egg (at room temperature)
2 tablespoons vegetable oil
Cornmeal

1. Combine 1 cup flour, sugar, yeast, and salt in a mixer bowl.
2. Stir in milk, egg, and oil; beat until smooth, about 3 minutes on high speed of electric mixer.
3. Stir in enough remaining flour to make a soft dough.
4. Turn out onto floured board; knead until smooth and elastic (5 to 8 minutes).
5. Cover with bowl; let rest 20 minutes.
6. Roll out to ½-inch thickness. Cut into 3- or 4-inch rounds. Sprinkle with cornmeal. Cover; let rise until double in bulk (about 45 minutes).
7. Bake in a greased heavy skillet or on a griddle on top of the range over low heat 20 to 30 minutes, or until golden brown, turning once. Cool and store in an airtight container or plastic bag.
8. To serve, split with knife or fork. Toast. Serve hot.

About 1 dozen muffins

Hurry-Up Dinner Rolls

2½ to 3 cups all-purpose flour
2 tablespoons sugar
1 package active dry yeast
½ teaspoon salt
¾ cup hot tap water (120° to 130°F)
1 egg (at room temperature)
2 tablespoons vegetable oil
2 tablespoons melted butter or
   margarine

1. Combine 1 cup flour, sugar, yeast, and salt in a bowl. Stir in water, egg, and oil; beat until smooth. Cover; let rise in a warm place 15 minutes.
2. Stir in enough remaining flour to make a soft, sticky dough.
3. Turn dough onto a floured board; continue to work in flour until dough can be kneaded. Knead until smooth and elastic (about 3 minutes).
4. Divide dough into 16 pieces; shape into balls. Place in a greased 9-inch square pan. Brush tops with melted butter. Cover; let rise 20 minutes.
5. Bake at 425°F 8 to 10 minutes.

16 rolls

Parmesan Bread Fingers

2½ cups all-purpose biscuit mix
1 package active dry yeast
½ teaspoon salt
⅔ cup hot water
¼ cup butter or margarine, melted
¼ cup grated Parmesan cheese

1. Combine biscuit mix, yeast, and salt in a bowl.
2. Stir in water until mixture clings to itself.
3. Turn dough onto a floured surface. Knead 8 to 10 times.
4. Roll out into a 13×9-inch rectangle.
5. Brush half of butter in a 13×9×2-inch baking pan. Place dough in pan, pressing to fit. Cut crosswise into 16 strips, then lengthwise in half.
6. Brush with remaining butter and sprinkle with cheese. Cover; let rise 15 minutes.
7. Bake at 425°F 15 minutes. Turn off oven; allow sticks to remain in oven 15 minutes.

32 bread fingers

Brooklyn Bagels

4 to 5 cups all-purpose flour
1 package active dry yeast
2 teaspoons salt
1½ cups hot water (120° to 130°F)
2 tablespoons honey or sugar
1 egg white
1 teaspoon water

1. Combine 1 cup flour, yeast, and salt in a bowl.
2. Stir in hot water and honey; beat until smooth, about 3 minutes. Stir in enough remaining flour to make a soft dough.
3. Turn out onto a floured surface; continue to work in flour until dough is stiff enough to knead. Knead until smooth and elastic (about 5 minutes).
4. Cover with bowl. Let rest 15 minutes.
5. Divide into 12 equal parts. Shape each into a flattened ball. With thumb and forefinger poke a hole into center. Stretch and rotate until hole enlarges to about 1 or 2 inches. Cover; let rise about 20 minutes.
6. Boil water in a large shallow pan, about 2 inches deep. Reduce heat. Simmer a few bagels at a time about 7 minutes. Remove from pan; drain on a towel about 5 minutes. Place on a baking sheet; brush with mixture of egg white and water.
7. Bake at 375°F 30 minutes, or until done.
8. To serve, split and toast. Spread with **butter** and **jam** or **cream cheese**.

1 dozen bagels

Serving your own warm sweet coffeecakes or rolls makes any breakfast or brunch a special affair.

From one basic sweet dough an abundance of flavorful things take form. By changing the shape or adding a variation of fillings, you have a new taste treat.

For those times when you want to have hot sweet rolls, but don't have the time to prepare them that day, use the Refrigerator Sweet Dough recipe. You can shape and refrigerate the dough 2 to 24 hours ahead and pull it out at the last minute. This gives you the chance to enjoy sleeping late.

Basic Sweet Dough

4 to 5 cups all-purpose flour
2 packages active dry yeast
1 teaspoon salt
¾ cup milk
½ cup water
½ cup melted butter
½ cup sugar
1 egg

1. Stir together 1¾ cups flour, yeast, and salt in a large mixer bowl.
2. Heat milk, water, butter, and sugar until very warm (120° to 130°F).
3. Add liquid ingredients to flour mixture; beat until smooth, about 2 minutes on electric mixer.
4. Add egg and ½ cup more flour and beat another 2 minutes.
5. Gradually add enough more flour to make a soft dough.
6. Turn out onto floured board; continue to work in flour until dough can be kneaded. Knead until smooth and elastic, but still soft (about 5 minutes).
7. Cover; let rest about 20 minutes.
8. Shape, let rise, and bake as directed in recipes that follow.

Cinnamon Rolls: Roll dough into a 13×9-inch rectangle. Spread with **2 tablespoons softened butter** or **margarine.** Sprinkle with mixture of **½ cup firmly packed brown** or **white sugar** and **2 teaspoons cinnamon.** Beginning with long side, roll dough up tightly jelly-roll fashion. Cut roll into 12 (1-inch) slices. Place slices in a greased 13×9×2-inch baking pan or greased muffin cups. Bake at 375°F 15 to 20 minutes.

1½ dozen

Glazed Raised Doughnuts: Follow recipe for Basic Sweet Dough. Roll out to about ½-inch thickness. Cut with doughnut cutter or make into shape of your choice, such as squares, twists, long johns, doughnut holes, or bismarcks. Let rise, uncovered, until light, 40 to 50 minutes. Fry in deep hot oil (375°F) 3 to 4 minutes, turning once. Drain on paper towels. Dip in a glaze of **1½ cups confectioners' sugar, 2 tablespoons warm water,** and **1 teaspoon vanilla extract.**

Apricot Crisscross Coffeecake: For one large coffeecake, roll dough into a 15×12-inch rectangle. For two small coffeecakes, divide dough in half. Roll each half into an 12×8-inch rectangle. Combine **½ cup apricot preserves, ½ cup raisins,** and **½ cup sliced almonds.** Spread half the filling lengthwise down the center of each rectangle. Make about 12 slashes, each 2 inches long, down the long sides of each coffeecake. Fold strips alternately over filling, herringbone fashion. Cover; let rise until double in bulk (50 to 60

Mushroom Bread, 24;
Potato Pan Rolls, 29;
Harvest Bread, 23

minutes). Bake at 375°F 20 to 25 minutes for small coffee-cakes and 35 to 40 minutes for large coffeecake.

Refrigerator Sweet Dough

      5 to 6 cups all-purpose flour
      2 packages active dry yeast
      ½ cup sugar
      1½ teaspoons salt
      1 cup milk
      ½ cup water
      ½ cup butter or margarine,
         softened
      2 eggs

1. Stir 1¾ cups flour, yeast, sugar, and salt together in a large mixer bowl.
2. Heat milk, water, and butter to very warm (120° to 130°F).
3. Add liquid to dry ingredients and beat until smooth, about 2 minutes on electric mixer.
4. Add eggs and ½ cup flour and continue beating another 2 minutes.
5. Gradually stir in enough additional flour to make a soft dough.
6. Turn out onto floured board; continue to work in flour until dough can be kneaded. Knead until smooth and elastic, but still soft (5 to 8 minutes).
7. Cover with plastic wrap, then with a towel.
8. Let rest 20 minutes.
9. Divide in half and shape as desired.
10. Brush with **oil.** Cover with plastic wrap.
11. Refrigerate 2 to 24 hours. When ready to bake, remove from refrigerator and let stand 10 minutes.
12. Bake at 375°F 20 to 30 minutes.
13. Remove from pans and cool on rack.

2 coffeecakes

Cinnamon Slice Coffeecake: Follow shaping instructions as in Cinnamon Rolls (page 32), only omit 13×9×2-inch pan. Instead, place 6 slices, cut-side down, on bottom of a greased 10-inch tube pan. Place 6 more slices cut-side against outer side of pan. Cover first layer with remaining 6 rolls. Bake at 375°F 20 to 25 minutes.

Cinnamon Discs: Combine ¾ cup firmly packed brown sugar, ¾ cup white sugar, ½ cup finely chopped pecans, and 1 teaspoon cinnamon. Divide dough in half. Roll each half into a 12-inch square. Melt ½ cup butter. Brush dough with 2 tablespoons of the butter. Sprinkle with ½ cup sugar mixture. Roll up jelly-roll fashion; pinch to seal edges. Cut into 1-inch slices. Place on greased baking sheets at least 3 inches apart. Cover with waxed paper. Flatten each to about 3 inches in diameter. Let rise 15 minutes. Flatten again. Brush with remaining butter; sprinkle with remaining sugar mixture. Cover with waxed paper; flatten again. Bake at 400°F 10 to 12 minutes.

2 dozen

Bubble Bread: Divide dough into 20 equal pieces; shape into balls. Combine ½ cup sugar or firmly packed brown sugar, ½ cup finely chopped nuts, and 1 teaspoon cinnamon. Melt ½ cup butter or margarine. Roll balls in butter, then in sugar mixture. Arrange balls in a well-greased 10-inch tube pan. Cover; let rise until double in bulk (45 to 60 minutes). Bake at 350°F 30 to 35 minutes.

(continued on page 34)

Orange Bubble Ring: Shape dough into 20 balls as for Bubble Bread. Roll each ball in **½ cup melted butter** and then a mixture of **½ cup sugar** and **1 tablespoon grated orange peel.** Arrange and bake as above.

Apricot Bubble Bread: Shape dough into 20 balls as for Bubble Bread; roll balls in butter, then in sugar. Arrange 10 balls in bottom of a well-greased 10-inch tube pan. Top with **¼ cup apricot preserves.** Repeat layers. Cover; let rise until double in bulk (about 45 minutes). Bake as directed.

Sweet Maple Coffeecake

3 to 3½ cups all-purpose flour
1 package active dry yeast
½ teaspoon salt
½ cup milk
¼ cup water
¼ cup butter or margarine
2 eggs
¼ cup honey or sugar
   Maple Filling

1. Combine 1 cup flour, yeast, and salt in a mixer bowl.
2. Warm milk, water, and butter in a small saucepan.
3. Add liquid, eggs, and honey to flour mixture; beat until smooth, about 3 minutes on electric mixer.
4. Stir in enough remaining flour to make a soft, sticky dough.
5. Turn out onto floured board; continue to work in flour until dough can be kneaded. Knead until smooth and elastic, but still soft (about 5 minutes).
6. Cover with a bowl; let rest 30 minutes.
7. Divide dough in half; roll each half into a 15×12-inch rectangle. Spread with Maple Filling. Fold each rectangle in thirds, making a 15×4-inch strip. Cut in 10 equal pieces. Place strips of dough in greased 8×4×2-inch loaf pans, cut side down. Cover; let rise 30 minutes.
8. Bake at 350°F 35 to 40 minutes.

2 loaves

Maple Filling: Cream ½ cup firmly packed brown sugar and ⅓ cup white sugar with ¼ cup softened butter or margarine. Stir in ¼ cup maple syrup, 2 tablespoons all-purpose flour, ½ teaspoon cinnamon, and ½ cup chopped nuts.

Nutty Sweet Twists

Now that you've mastered the basic yeast dough, you're ready for a new twist!

1 can (13 ounces) evaporated milk
   or 1⅔ cups milk
1 tablespoon lemon juice or
   vinegar
½ cup raisins
3 tablespoons sugar
2 tablespoons butter or margarine
3 to 3¼ cups all-purpose flour
1 package active dry yeast

1. Warm milk and lemon juice in a small saucepan. Add raisins, sugar, and 2 tablespoons butter.
2. Combine 2 cups flour, yeast, salt, and baking soda in a large mixer bowl. Stir in milk mixture and egg; beat until smooth.
3. Stir in enough remaining flour to make a soft, sticky dough.
4. Turn out onto a floured surface; continue to work in flour until dough can be kneaded. Knead until smooth and elastic,

1 teaspoon salt
½ teaspoon baking soda
1 egg
2 tablespoons butter or margarine,
    softened or melted
⅓ cup firmly packed brown sugar
⅓ cup finely chopped nuts
2 teaspoons cinnamon

but still soft (about 5 minutes). Let dough rest 5 minutes.

5. Roll dough into a 24×12-inch rectangle, about ⅛ inch thick. Spread or brush with 2 tablespoons butter. Sprinkle with a mixture of brown sugar, nuts, and cinnamon. Fold in half lengthwise, forming a 24×6-inch rectangle. Cut into 1-inch strips. For each roll, hold both ends of strip and twist. Place on greased baking sheet. (If shorter rolls are desired, cut twists in half.)

6. Bake at 375°F 10 to 15 minutes (see Note).

*2 dozen long (6-inch) twists
or 4 dozen short (3-inch) twists*

Note: For shinier twists, brush dough with mixture of **1 egg white** and **1 teaspoon water** just before baking.

Frosted Sweet Twists: Follow recipe for Nutty Sweet Twists and glaze baked rolls with a mixture of **½ cup confectioners' sugar** and **1 tablespoon milk.**

Austrian Almond Braid

5 to 5½ cups all-purpose flour
2 packages active dry yeast
1 cup milk
½ cup sugar
½ cup shortening or butter
¼ cup water
2 teaspoons salt
2 eggs (at room temperature)
½ cup golden raisins
½ cup candied mixed fruit, chopped
½ cup chopped blanched almonds
    Almond Icing (see recipe)
    Candied fruit and nuts for
        decoration (optional)

1. Combine 2 cups flour and yeast in a large mixer bowl.

2. Heat milk, sugar, shortening, water, and salt in a saucepan over low heat until very warm (120° to 130°F), stirring to blend. Add liquid to flour-yeast mixture and beat until smooth, about 3 minutes on medium speed of electric mixer. Blend in eggs. Add 1 cup flour and beat 1 minute. Stir in fruit and almonds; add more flour to make a soft dough.

3. Turn dough onto a lightly floured surface; knead until smooth and satiny (5 to 10 minutes). Cover dough and let rest 20 minutes. Divide dough in half.

4. For each braid, take two-thirds of one portion of dough and divide into thirds. Roll each piece with hands into a 15-inch strand. Braid strands on lightly greased baking sheet. Divide remaining third into thirds; form three 18-inch strands. Braid strands loosely; place on first braid, pressing in lightly. Tuck ends of top braid under ends of bottom braid. Brush with oil. Let rise in a warm place until double in bulk (about 45 minutes).

5. Bake at 350°F 25 to 30 minutes, or until golden brown. Remove from baking sheets to wire rack. While braids are still slightly warm, ice with almond icing. Decorate with candied fruit and nuts, if desired.

2 large loaves

Almond Icing: Put **1½ cups confectioners' sugar, 2 tablespoons milk,** and **1 teaspoon almond extract** into a small bowl; stir until smooth.

Sally Lunn

5 cups all-purpose flour
½ cup sugar
1 package active dry yeast
1 teaspoon salt
1½ cups milk
½ cup butter or margarine
3 eggs
¼ cup sugar
¼ teaspoon nutmeg

1. Combine 2 cups flour, ½ cup sugar, yeast, and salt in a mixer bowl.
2. Heat milk and butter in a small saucepan.
3. Add liquid with eggs to flour mixture; beat 2 minutes by hand or with electric mixer.
4. Stir in remaining flour by hand. Cover; let rise until double in bulk (about 1 hour).
5. Stir dough down. Pour into a greased and sugared 10-inch tube pan. Cover; let rise until double in bulk (about 30 minutes).
6. Combine ¼ cup sugar and nutmeg; sprinkle over dough.
7. Bake at 400°F 40 minutes. Cool in pan 5 minutes.
8. If desired, serve hot with strawberries and whipped cream.

One large loaf

Russian Kulich

5 cups all-purpose flour
2 packages active dry yeast
1 cup milk
½ cup sugar
¼ cup oil
2 teaspoons salt
2 eggs (at room temperature)
2 teaspoons grated lemon peel
½ cup chopped blanched almonds
¼ cup raisins
¼ cup chopped candied citron
¼ cup chopped candied orange peel
¼ cup chopped candied cherries
½ cup confectioners' sugar
1 tablespoon milk
  Candied fruit (optional)

1. Combine 1 cup flour and yeast in a large mixer bowl.
2. Heat 1 cup milk, sugar, oil, and salt in a saucepan over low heat until very warm (120° to 130°F), stirring to blend. Add liquid to flour-yeast mixture and beat until smooth, about 2 minutes on medium speed of electric mixer. Beat in eggs, lemon peel, almonds, raisins, and candied fruit. Add 1 cup flour and beat 1 minute on medium speed. Stir in more flour to make a soft dough.
3. Turn dough onto a lightly floured surface and knead until smooth and satiny (8 to 10 minutes). Shape into a ball and place in a lightly greased bowl; turn to grease surface. Cover; let rise in a warm place until double in bulk (about 1½ hours).
4. Punch dough down; divide into 2 or 3 equal portions and shape into balls. Let rest 10 minutes.
5. Grease generously two 46-ounce juice cans or three 1-pound coffee cans. Place dough in cans, filling about half full; brush with oil. Let rise until double in bulk (about 1 hour).
6. Bake at 350°F 30 to 35 minutes, or until golden brown. Immediately remove from cans and cool.
7. Blend confectioners' sugar and 1 tablespoon milk until smooth; ice top of loaves. Decorate with candied fruit, if desired.

2 large or 3 medium loaves

QUICK BREADS

Quick breads are the answer for the person who wants to have homemade breads but who doesn't have a lot of time. They are the easiest and quickest to prepare and can be served anywhere, anytime. They can be taken along on picnics, served at breakfast or dinner, eaten for late night snacks.

The ingredients are similar for all quick breads, but they produce different products depending on the differing amounts used and how they are mixed or baked or cooked.

These breads are "quick" because they are not leavened by yeast, which takes time to grow and expand the dough. Biscuits, pancakes, short-cakes, loaves are all leavened by baking powder or baking soda. Steam makes cream puffs or popover puff into shape. The amount of liquid determines whether a batter can be poured, dropped, spread, or kneaded.

There are standard methods used to make each type of quick bread. Once you become acquainted with these simple basic steps, you can improvise and add your own special touches.

MUFFIN METHOD:

1. Sift or stir all the dry ingredients in a mixing bowl. Make a "well" or a depression in the center.
2. Add the liquid (milk, eggs, oil) all at once and stir only until the dry ingredients are moistened. It should still look lumpy. Overmixing at this point will produce a tough muffin with tunnels, peaks, and cracks.

BISCUIT METHOD:

1. Stir dry ingredients together in a mixing bowl.
2. Cut the shortening into the flour mixture with a pastry blender or 2 knives until it is crumbly and the fat is evenly distributed.
3. Add the liquid and stir until just blended. To avoid over mixing, push flour away from the sides of the bowl into the center to dampen.
4. At this point the dough may be either kneaded gently about ½ minute and rolled or patted ½ inch thick and then cut into biscuits, or it may be simply patted in a shallow pan for a different texture.

Note: The cutting-in of the fat is what gives biscuits their customary flaky tenderness.

Quick bread loaves are a little like wine—they improve with age. If you can resist eating it right from the oven, the flavors in the bread will have mellowed a day later and be more pronounced. The loaf is also easier to slice.

These breads are mixed like a cake. Two methods are generally used in recipes: the conventional or traditional method, and the modified version, which is quicker.

CONVENTIONAL METHOD:

1. Cream the shortening until it is light and fluffy, to incorporate air into the batter.
2. Beat in the eggs.
3. Add the dry ingredients alternately with the liquid, beating well after each addition.

MODIFIED ONE-BOWL METHOD:

1. Cream the shortening, sugar, eggs, and liquids all at the same time.
2. Stir in the dry ingredients.

Quick bread loaves have a cakelike texture because of the

high proportion of fat and sugar. A usual characteristic of the loaf is an open crack down the center of the loaf.

To tell when bread is done, insert a wooden pick into the center; it will come out clean. The bread should be golden brown. Cool completely on a rack before wrapping. Wrapped quick breads will keep for several days, if you are lucky enough to keep them from disappearing before then.

Quick Buttermilk Bread

1¾ cups all-purpose flour
2 teaspoons baking powder
¾ teaspoon baking soda
1 teaspoon salt
⅓ cup firmly packed brown sugar
1½ cups uncooked oats
1 cup buttermilk
½ cup vegetable oil
2 eggs, beaten
½ cup chopped pecans

1. Mix flour, baking powder, baking soda, and salt in a bowl. Stir in brown sugar and oats. Add remaining ingredients; stir only until dry ingredients are moistened.
2. Pour batter into a greased 9×5×3-inch loaf pan.
3. Bake at 350°F 50 to 55 minutes. Cool on wire rack about 10 minutes. Remove from pan; cool thoroughly.
4. Wrap and store. (Bread will slice better if stored a day before slicing.)

1 loaf

Cheddar Cornbread

1 cup yellow cornmeal
1 cup all-purpose flour
1 tablespoon baking powder
1 teaspoon salt
2 cups shredded Cheddar cheese (8 ounces)
1 cup milk
¼ cup melted butter or margarine or vegetable oil
1 egg
4 slices crisply cooked bacon, crumbled
1 green pepper, sliced (optional)

1. Combine cornmeal, flour, baking powder, salt, and 1 cup cheese in a mixing bowl.
2. Combine milk, butter, and egg in a separate bowl; beat well.
3. Add liquid ingredients to dry ingredients; stir just until flour is moistened. Pour into a greased 9-inch round layer cake pan. Sprinkle with remaining cheese and bacon. Top with green pepper rings, if desired.
4. Bake at 425°F 25 minutes, or until done.

About 8 servings

Pleasin' Pumpkin Bread

3½ cups all-purpose flour
3 cups sugar
2 cups cooked mashed pumpkin
1 cup vegetable oil
⅓ cup water
4 eggs
2 teaspoons baking soda
1½ teaspoons salt
2 teaspoons cinnamon
½ teaspoon nutmeg
¼ teaspoon cloves
¼ teaspoon ginger

1. Put flour, sugar, baking soda, salt, and spices into a large mixing bowl; mix well. Add pumpkin, oil, water, and eggs; beat until well blended.
2. Divide batter equally into 2 greased 9×5×3-inch loaf pans.
3. Bake at 350°F 70 minutes, or until done.
4. Cool before wrapping.

2 loaves

Buttermilk Coffee Cake

1 cup sugar
½ cup butter or margarine, soften
2 eggs
1 teaspoon vanilla extract
2 cups all-purpose flour
1 teaspoon baking powder
1 teaspoon baking soda
½ teaspoon salt
1 cup buttermilk

Topping:
1 cup chopped nuts
1 cup sugar
⅓ cup firmly packed br   ar
1 teaspoon cinnamor
½ cup butter or marg

1. Cream sugar and butter; beat in eggs and vanilla extract until well blended.
2. Combine flour, baking powder, baking soda, and salt.
3. Add buttermilk and flour mixture alternately to sugar mixture, beating well after each addition.
4. For topping, combine nuts, sugar, brown sugar, and cinnamon. Cut in butter.
5. Sprinkle half of topping mixture in bottom of a greased and floured 13×9×2-inch baking pan. Pour in batter. Cover with remaining topping.
6. Bake at 350°F 25 to 30 minutes.
7. Serve warm.

1 coffeecake

Rhubarb   l

1½ cups firmly   sugar
⅔ cup veget
1 cup butt
1 egg
1 teaspo   xtract
2½ cups   flour
1 teas   t
1 tea   n baking soda
1½ cv   nely chopped rhubarb
½ c hopped nuts
2   spoons sugar

1. Beat brown sugar, oil, buttermilk, egg, and vanilla extract in a mixing bowl.
2. Mix flour, salt, and baking soda. Add to brown sugar mixture and stir until blended.
3. Stir in rhubarb and nuts.
4. Turn into 2 greased 8×4×2-inch loaf pans. Sprinkle 1 tablespoon sugar over each.
5. Bake at 325°F 1 hour, or until done.

2 loaves

Zucchini Bread

2 cups sugar
1 cup vegetable oil
3 eggs
1 teaspoon vanilla extract
3 cups all-purpose flour
1 teaspoon salt
1 teaspoon baking soda
1 teaspoon cinnamon
2 cups shredded unpeeled zucchini
1 cup chopped nuts

1. Beat sugar, oil, eggs, and vanilla extract in a mixing bowl until fluffy.
2. Mix flour, salt, baking soda, and cinnamon. Add to egg mixture and stir until blended.
3. Stir in zucchini and nuts.
4. Turn into a greased 9×5×3-inch loaf pan.
5. Bake at 350°F 1 hour and 20 minutes, or until done.
6. Cool before wrapping.

1 loaf

Oklahoma Oatmeal Bread

1 cup evaporated milk
2 tablespoons vegetable oil
1 tablespoon vinegar
1 cup uncooked oats
1 cup all-purpose flour
1 cup firmly packed brown sugar
1 teaspoon baking soda
½ teaspoon salt
1 cup raisins or chopped nuts

1. Beat milk, oil, and vinegar in a mixing bowl until smooth.
2. Add oats, flour, brown sugar, baking soda, and salt; mix until well blended.
3. Stir in raisins or nuts.
4. Turn into a greased 9×5×3-inch loaf pan or two 7×4×2-inch loaf pans.
5. Bake at 350°F 50 to 60 minutes, or until done.
6. Cool before wrapping.

1 large loaf or 2 small loaves

Light, flaky biscuits are a snap to make. They can be mixed minutes before the meal and served piping hot right from the oven.

The same biscuit dough can be either rolled or dropped onto a baking sheet, depending on your preference and time. Drop biscuits are dropped by spoonfuls onto a greased baking sheet just like a cookie. Then you pop them into the oven. To produce that wonderful flakiness and shape typical of the rolled biscuit, an additional step must be taken. The dough is gently kneaded about ½ minute, rolled or patted out, and cut with a biscuit cutter. Both kinds are baked in a hot (425°-450°F) oven 10 to 12 minutes.

A technique to remember to get straight, even sides is to push the biscuit cutter evenly, straight down, without twisting. If you like soft sides, place the biscuits close together in a shallow pan. For crusty sides, allow about an inch around each biscuit on the baking sheet.

To pull piping-hot, mouth-watering biscuits out of the oven just as everyone is sitting down to dinner or breakfast, you can cheat a little on the time schedule. Prepare the biscuits, put on a baking sheet, and cover with plastic wrap. Refrigerate up to one hour before you are ready to bake. Just allow a few extra minutes for them to bake.

Biscuits

2 cups all-purpose flour
1 tablespoon baking powder
1 teaspoon salt
⅓ cup butter or shortening
¾ cup milk

1. Combine flour, baking powder, and salt in a mixing bowl. Cut in butter with pastry blender or 2 knives until mixture resembles rice kernels.
2. Stir in milk with a fork just until mixture clings to itself.
3. Form dough into a ball and knead gently 8 to 10 times on lightly floured board. Gently roll dough ½ inch thick.
4. Cut with floured biscuit cutter or knife, using an even pressure to keep sides of biscuits straight.
5. Place on ungreased baking sheet, close together for soft-sided biscuits or 1 inch apart for crusty ones.
6. Bake at 450°F 10 to 15 minutes, or until golden brown.

About 1 dozen

Southern Buttermilk Biscuits: Follow recipe for Biscuits, substituting **buttermilk** for the milk and adding ¼ teaspoon baking soda to the dry ingredients and reducing baking powder to 2 teaspoons.

Drop Biscuits: Follow recipe for Biscuits, increasing milk to 1 cup. Omit rolling-out instructions. Simply drop from a spoon onto a lightly greased baking sheet.

Scones

1²⁄₃ cups all-purpose flour
  1 tablespoon sugar
1½ teaspoons baking powder
  ½ teaspoon baking soda
  ½ teaspoon salt
  ½ cup shortening
  ½ cup buttermilk

1. Combine flour, sugar, baking powder, baking soda, and salt in a mixing bowl. Cut in shortening with pastry blender or two knives until mixture resembles rice kernels.
2. Stir in buttermilk with a fork until mixture clings to itself.
3. Form dough into a ball and knead gently about 8 times on a floured surface. Divide dough in half; roll each into a round about ½ inch thick. Cut each round into 6 wedge-shaped pieces. Place on ungreased baking sheets.
4. Bake at 450°F 8 to 10 minutes. Serve warm.

1 dozen

Savory Biscuit Bread

1½ cups all-purpose flour
  1 tablespoon baking powder
  ½ teaspoon salt
  ½ teaspoon paprika
  ½ teaspoon celery salt
  ¼ teaspoon pepper
  ¼ teaspoon poultry seasoning
  ¼ cup shortening
  ½ cup milk (about)

1. Combine flour, baking powder, and seasonings in a mixing bowl. Cut in shortening until mixture resembles rice kernels.
2. Stir in milk with a fork just until flour is moistened.
3. Pat into a greased 8-inch round layer cake pan.
4. Bake at 450°F 10 to 15 minutes, or until done.

6 servings

Muffins are a variety show in themselves. They fit in anywhere because they can be sweet or not, they can be chock full of goodies for hearty eating or simply appetite teasers, or be petite or jumbo in size.

The trick of making perfect muffins is in mixing the dry ingredients with the liquids until just moistened. This is the one time when the batter is supposed to look lumpy. Perfect muffins have a rounded, shiny, pebbled, golden brown crust. The inside will be moist, light, tender, and even textured.

Dakota Bran Muffins

  1 cup all-purpose flour
  1 tablespoon baking powder
  ½ teaspoon salt
1½ cups ready-to-eat bran flakes
  1 cup milk
  1 egg
  ¼ cup vegetable oil
  ¼ cup honey or sugar

1. Combine dry ingredients in a mixing bowl.
2. Combine remaining ingredients in a separate bowl; beat well.
3. Add liquid ingredients to dry ingredients; stir just until flour is moistened. Spoon batter into 12 greased muffin-pan wells.
4. Bake at 400°F 20 to 25 minutes, or until golden brown.

1 dozen

Sunshine Corn Muffins

1½ cups all-purpose flour
1½ cups yellow cornmeal
1 tablespoon baking powder
⅛ teaspoon salt
1 cup milk
½ cup honey
½ cup vegetable oil
2 eggs

1. Combine dry ingredients in a mixing bowl.
2. Combine remaining ingredients in a separate bowl; beat well.
3. Add liquid ingredients to dry ingredients; stir just until flour is moistened. Spoon into 24 greased muffin-pan wells.
4. Bake at 400°F 15 to 20 minutes, or until wooden pick inserted in muffin comes out clean.

2 dozen

Sunshine Cornbread: Follow recipe for Sunshine Corn Muffins, except pour mixture into a greased 9-inch square pan. Bake at 400°F 30 minutes, or until done.

6 servings

Lemon Chiffon Muffins

½ cup softened butter or margarine
½ cup sugar
   Grated peel of 1 lemon (about 1 tablespoon)
2 tablespoons milk
2 eggs, separated
3 tablespoons lemon juice (about 1 lemon)
1 cup all-purpose flour
1 teaspoon baking powder
¼ teaspoon salt
¼ cup chopped nuts
1 tablespoon sugar
1 teaspoon nutmeg

1. Cream butter, sugar, lemon peel, milk, and egg yolks in a mixing bowl until light and fluffy. Beat in lemon juice.
2. Combine flour, baking powder, and salt in a separate bowl. Add to batter and mix just until blended.
3. Beat egg whites until soft peaks form; fold into batter.
4. Spoon into 12 greased muffin-pan wells. Sprinkle with a mixture of nuts, sugar, and nutmeg.
5. Bake at 375°F 15 to 20 minutes, or until done.

1 dozen

Maple Tree Muffins

2 cups all-purpose flour
1 tablespoon baking powder
½ teaspoon salt
½ cup chopped nuts
⅔ cup milk
½ cup pure maple syrup or maple-blended syrup
1 egg
¼ cup vegetable oil

1. Combine flour, baking powder, salt, and nuts in a mixing bowl.
2. Combine remaining ingredients in a separate bowl; beat well.
3. Add liquid ingredients to dry ingredients; stir just until flour is moistened. Spoon into 12 greased muffin-pan wells.
4. Bake at 400°F 15 to 20 minutes, or until a wooden pick inserted in muffin comes out clean.

1 dozen

Bran-Oatmeal Muffins

¾ cup bran cereal
¾ cup milk
¼ cup butter or margarine
¼ cup molasses
1 egg
1 cup all-purpose flour

1. Combine bran cereal and milk to soften.
2. Beat butter and molasses together in a bowl. Add egg and mix well. Add bran-milk mixture.
3. Mix flour, sugar, baking powder, baking soda, and salt. Add dry ingredients to bran mixture; stir just until moistened. Stir in oats.

2 tablespoons sugar
1 teaspoon baking powder
½ teaspoon baking soda
½ teaspoon salt
1 cup uncooked oats

4. Spoon mixture into 12 greased medium-sized muffin-pan wells.
5. Bake at 400°F 15 to 18 minutes, or until golden brown.

1 dozen

Pancakes and waffles from a simple batter make possible a delicious array of combinations. Pancakes can be rolled, stuffed, or stacked with creamed meats or vegetables or sweet syrups for breakfast through dinner. You can add chopped nuts, raisins, coconut, fruits, and herbs to change the basic batter.

Two things to remember to make perfect pancakes or waffles. The batter should not be overmixed and the temperature of the griddle must be right. The dry ingredients are stirred with the liquid until just blended, and the batter should still be lumpy. You can make pancakes just how you like them, either thick or thin, by adding more or less liquid to the recipe.

The griddle is hot enough for baking when drops of cold water sprinkled on the surface dance in small beads.

Pancakes

1½ cups sifted all-purpose flour
1 tablespoon sugar
1½ teaspoons baking powder
¼ teaspoon salt
2 egg yolks, beaten
1⅓ cups milk
2 tablespoons butter or margarine, melted
2 egg whites

1. Start heating griddle or heavy skillet over low heat.
2. Mix flour, sugar, baking powder, and salt in a bowl.
3. Combine egg yolks, milk, and butter. Add liquid to flour mixture and beat until blended.
4. Beat egg whites until rounded peaks are formed. Spread beaten egg whites over batter and fold gently together.
5. Test griddle; it is hot enough for baking when drops of water sprinkled on surface dance in small beads. Lightly grease griddle, if so directed by manufacturer.
6. Pour batter onto griddle into pools about 4 inches in diameter, leaving at least 1 inch between cakes. Turn pancakes as they become puffy and full of bubbles. Turn only once.
7. Serve hot.

About 12 pancakes

Buttermilk Pancakes: Follow recipe for Pancakes; substitute **½ teaspoon baking soda** for the baking powder and **buttermilk** for the milk. Do not separate eggs. Beat eggs with buttermilk and proceed as in step 3 above.

Cornmeal Pancakes: Follow recipe for Pancakes. Decrease flour to ¾ cup. Mix **¾ cup yellow cornmeal** into dry ingredients.

Rye Pancakes: Follow recipe for Buttermilk Pancakes. Decrease flour to ¾ cup and mix in **¾ cup rye flour.** Blend **3 tablespoons molasses** into buttermilk-egg mixture.

Blueberry Pancakes: Follow recipe for Pancakes; gently fold **2 cups rinsed and drained blueberries** into batter after folding in beaten egg whites.

Waffles

2 cups sifted all-purpose flour
1 tablespoon sugar
1 tablespoon baking powder
½ teaspoon salt
3 eggs, well beaten
2 cups milk
½ cup butter or margarine, melted

1. Mix flour, sugar, baking powder, and salt in a bowl.
2. Combine eggs, milk, and melted butter. Add liquid mixture to flour mixture; beat just until batter is blended.
3. Heat waffle baker. Pour enough batter into waffle baker to allow spreading to within 1 inch of edges. Lower cover and bake waffle; do not raise cover during baking. Lift cover and loosen waffle with a fork. Serve hot.

About 4 large waffles

Buttermilk Waffles: Follow recipe for Waffles; substitute **buttermilk** for milk. Decrease baking powder to 2 teaspoons and add **1 teaspoon baking soda**.

Wheat Germ Pecan Waffles: Follow recipe for Waffles; decrease flour to 1½ cups. Stir **½ cup toasted wheat germ** into the flour mixture. Sprinkle **3 tablespoons coarsely chopped pecans** onto the batter before baking each waffle.

Cheese Waffles: Follow recipe for Waffles. When batter is smooth, blend in **½ cup shredded cheese**.

Chocolate Waffles: Follow recipe for Waffles. Generously sprinkle **semisweet chocolate pieces** over batter before closing waffle baker.

Popovers, unlike the other quick breads, rely on steam as the leavening agent. (The others use baking powder or baking soda.) The steam is produced from the high amount of liquid present in popover batter. It is this steam that gives the popover its characteristic hollow interior. The crispy outside structure comes from eggs and gluten. If they turn out any other way, they just aren't popovers.

Failure of popovers to "pop" is probably due to one of two reasons. One is underbeating. The batter should be beaten vigorously to develop the gluten. The second reason may be the oven temperature. It must be hot enough to achieve a sudden rise to open up the inside of the popover.

Popovers

3 eggs
1 cup milk
2 tablespoons vegetable oil
½ teaspoon salt
1 cup sifted all-purpose flour

1. Beat eggs in a mixing bowl. Beat in milk, oil, and salt.
2. Beat in flour until mixture is smooth and well blended.
3. For best results, preheat iron popover pan after thoroughly coating pan wells with shortening or oil. Pour batter into 8 popover-pan wells or 8 greased heat-resistant custard cups.
4. Bake at 400°F 35 to 40 minutes, or until popovers are puffed and golden brown. Serve hot with butter.

8 popovers

Note: For a crispier popover, make slit in side of each baked popover to allow the steam to escape. Return popovers to oven for 10 minutes with the heat turned off.

Jiffy quick breads from convenience foods give you a head start on the road to home baking. Some of the following recipes use a biscuit mix which has the fat and leavening agents already preblended for you. Because most of them are mixed all in one bowl and then baked, you can enjoy hot, homemade breads in a twinkling.

Homemade Croutons

Day-old bread slices
Softened butter or margarine

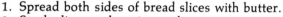

1. Spread both sides of bread slices with butter.
2. Stack slices and cut into cubes.
3. Spread over baking sheet.
4. Bake at 275°F 25 to 35 minutes, stirring occasionally, until dry and lightly browned.

Parmesan Croutons: Follow recipe for Homemade Croutons, except sprinkle both sides of bread with **grated Parmesan cheese** before cubing and baking.

Crusty Croutons: Follow recipe for Homemade Croutons except use **French bread** slices instead of day-old bread slices and do not cube bread. Turn slices over once during baking.

Poppy Seed Cheese Bread

1 cup shredded Cheddar cheese (4 ounces)
1 cup all-purpose biscuit mix
⅓ cup milk
1 egg
¼ cup chopped onion
1 tablespoon poppy seed

1. Combine ½ cup cheese and biscuit mix in a mixing bowl.
2. Add milk; stir just until flour is moistened. Pat dough over bottom of a greased 8- or 9-inch pie plate.
3. Combine remaining cheese, egg, and onion. Spread over biscuit dough. Sprinkle with poppy seed.
4. Bake at 425°F 15 to 20 minutes.

About 6 servings

Sesame Seed Twists

2 cups biscuit mix
¼ cup chilled butter
3 tablespoons melted butter
2 tablespoons sesame seed
1 egg yolk
1 teaspoon milk

1. Prepare biscuit mix as directed on package for rolled biscuits. Roll out on a lightly floured surface into a 12-inch square.
2. Thinly slice 3 tablespoons of butter and place on half of dough; fold other half over it. With rolling pin, gently seal open edges. Repeat procedure, using remaining chilled butter. Fold other half over, forming a 6-inch square.
3. Roll dough into a 12-inch square. Divide in half. Set one half in refrigerator.
4. Brush surface with melted butter. Sprinkle with some of the sesame seed. Cut into twelve 6×1-inch strips. Twist each strip and place on an ungreased baking sheet. Brush with mixture of egg yolk and milk. Sprinkle with more sesame seed. Repeat with other half.
5. Bake at 425°F 10 minutes.

2 dozen twists

Quick Strips

1 loaf unsliced white bread
½ cup butter or margarine, melted
¼ teaspoon garlic salt
Grated Parmesan cheese, sesame seed, or poppy seed

1. Cut four 1¼-inch slices from loaf of bread. Cut each slice into 1-inch strips.
2. Combine butter and garlic salt in a 13×9×2-inch baking pan.
3. Toss bread strips in butter; sprinkle with cheese.
4. Bake at 350°F 20 minutes.

About 20 strips

Garlic Bread

1 loaf French bread
½ cup butter or margarine, softened
¼ teaspoon garlic powder or garlic salt

1. Slice bread almost through to bottom crust at 1-inch intervals.
2. Thoroughly combine butter and garlic powder. Spread on both sides of each bread slice.
3. Place on baking sheet.
4. Bake at 350°F 15 to 20 minutes, or until hot and crispy.

About 1 dozen slices

La Verde Slices

1 loaf Italian bread, cut diagonally in 1-inch slices
½ cup softened butter or margarine
2 tablespoons finely chopped green pepper
2 tablespoons finely chopped onion

1. Broil bread slices until golden brown on each side.
2. Combine butter, green pepper, and onion. Spread on one side of each slice.
3. Broil until lightly browned.

About 1 dozen slices

Sugar Buns

1 cup firmly packed brown sugar
⅓ cup butter or margarine
1 tablespoon corn syrup
½ cup chopped pecans
2 cans refrigerated dough for butterflake dinner rolls

1. Combine brown sugar, butter, and corn syrup in a saucepan; bring to boiling, stirring occasionally.
2. Stir in pecans.
3. Divide mixture evenly among 12 muffin-pan wells.
4. Place 2 rolls in each cup.
5. Bake at 375°F 15 minutes. Remove from pans immediately.

1 dozen buns

Cranberry Swirl Rolls

1 package (about 14 ounces) hot roll mix
1 can (16 ounces) jellied cranberry sauce
¼ cup firmly packed brown sugar
1 teaspoon cinnamon

1. Prepare hot roll mix following package directions.
2. Roll half of dough at a time into a 12×8-inch rectangle. Spread each rectangle with cranberry sauce to within 1 inch of edge. Sprinkle with brown sugar and cinnamon. Starting with a 12-inch side, roll up jelly-roll fashion. Seal edges. Cut each into 1-inch slices and place cut-side down on greased baking sheets.
3. Bake at 375°F 10 minutes, or until done.

About 2 dozen rolls

Cinnamon Swirl Date Ring

  3 **cups all-purpose biscuit mix**
¼ **cup sugar**
¼ **cup butter or margarine**
¾ **cup milk**
    Cinnamon-Date Filling

1. Combine biscuit mix and sugar in a mixing bowl; cut in butter until mixture resembles rice kernels.
2. Gently stir in milk just until ingredients are moistened.
3. Drop half of dough by tablespoonfuls into a greased 6-cup ring mold. Sprinkle with Cinnamon-Date Filling. Top with remaining dough.
4. Bake at 350°F 25 to 30 minutes, or until a wooden pick inserted in cake comes out clean. Invert mold onto plate; leave over cake 5 minutes. Serve warm.

One coffeecake ring

Cinnamon-Date Filling: Combine **½ cup melted butter or margarine, ½ cup chopped dates, ¼ cup chopped nuts,** and **1 teaspoon cinnamon.**

Doughnuts are more than a sweet treat during coffee breaks; they help bring people together for enjoyable conversations and can even be the whole reason for the party.

Fry cakes, as they are sometimes called, can be rolled and cut into shapes, or dropped by spoonfuls into the hot fat. In both cases the temperature of the fat is very important. The fat should be heated slowly and be maintained at 375°F throughout the cooking. If the temperature is too low, the dough will soak up too much fat; if it is too hot, the outside will brown before the inside has completely cooked.

Pour in enough oil or fat to half fill a 3- to 4-quart saucepan. This leaves enough room for the bubbling action of the doughnuts cooking.

It is helpful to have a wire basket or slotted spoon to remove the doughnuts from the oil to absorbent paper to drain.

Lemon Doughnut Balls

  2 **cups all-purpose flour**
¼ **cup sugar**
  1 **tablespoon baking powder**
  1 **teaspoon salt**
½ **teaspoon baking soda**
½ **cup milk**
¼ **cup melted butter or margarine**
  2 **tablespoons grated lemon peel**
¼ **cup lemon juice**
  1 **egg**
½ **cup flaked coconut**
    **Vegetable oil or shortening
      heated to 375°F**
    Confectioners' sugar

1. Combine flour, sugar, baking powder, salt, and baking soda in a mixing bowl.
2. Combine milk, butter, lemon peel and juice, egg, and coconut in a separate bowl; beat well.
3. Add liquid ingredients to dry ingredients. Stir just until flour is moistened.
4. Drop by teaspoonfuls into hot oil. Fry 3 minutes, or until golden brown. Drain on paper towels. Sprinkle with confectioners' sugar.

About 3 dozen

Filled Berlin Doughnuts *(Bismarcks)*

A hint of orange and rum extract flavors these puffy Bismarcks. Fill them with your favorite jelly.

1 package active dry yeast
¼ cup warm water
½ cup sugar
1 teaspoon salt
⅓ cup butter
1 tablespoon orange juice
2 teaspoons rum extract
1 cup milk, scalded
3½ to 4 cups all-purpose flour
2 eggs, well beaten
Fat for deep frying heated to 375°F
Jam or jelly

1. Soften yeast in the warm water.
2. Put ½ cup sugar, the salt, butter, orange juice and rum extract into a large bowl. Pour scalded milk over ingredients in bowl. Stir until butter is melted. Cool to lukewarm.
3. Blend in 1 cup of the flour and beat until smooth. Stir in yeast. Add about half of the remaining flour and beat until smooth. Beat in the eggs. Then beat in enough of the remaining flour to make a soft dough.
4. Turn dough onto a lightly floured surface and let rest 5 to 10 minutes.
5. Knead until smooth and elastic. Form into a ball and put into a greased deep bowl; turn dough to bring greased surface to top. Cover; let rise in a warm place until double in bulk.
6. Punch down dough. Turn dough onto a lightly floured surface and roll ½ inch thick. Cut dough into rounds with a 3-inch cutter. Cover with waxed paper and let rise on rolling surface away from drafts and direct heat, until double in bulk (30 to 45 minutes).
7. About 20 minutes before deep frying, heat fat.
8. Fry doughnuts in heated fat. Put in only as many doughnuts at one time as will float uncrowded one layer deep in the fat. Fry 2 to 3 minutes, or until lightly browned; turn doughnuts with a fork or tongs when they rise to the surface and several times during cooking (do not pierce). Lift from fat; drain over fat for a few seconds before removing to absorbent paper. Cool.
9. Cut a slit through to the center in the side of each doughnut. Force about ½ teaspoon jam or jelly into center and press lightly to close slit. (A pastry bag and tube may be used to force jelly or jam into slit.) Shake 2 or 3 Bismarcks at one time in bag containing **sugar.**

About 2 dozen

BREAD WITH SOUP

THE INTERNATIONAL SET

If you can't travel around the world to discover its gastronomic delights, then you can create those international dishes in your own kitchen. Each country has its distinctive foods and food customs for which it is best known.

The olive trees in Greece dictate what some of its national dishes will include. The fish and dairy products of the Scandinavian countries reflect their creative use of these products in smorgasbords. Hungarians use spices to uniquely flavor their foods and curry dominates Indian cookery—the list is endless.

Imaginative national dishes can range from haute cuisine to hearty informal fare. Selected in this section are bread and soup recipes that will allow you to bring a foreign culture into your life.

Greek Egg-Lemon Soup

Lemons are to Greece as oranges are to Florida—they just can't seem to get enough of them. And this soup is as common to them as chicken-noodle is to Americans.

6 cups rich veal or chicken broth (page 62) or 6 bouillon cubes in 6 cups water
⅓ cup uncooked rice
3 eggs
¼ cup lemon juice

1. Bring broth to boiling in a large saucepan. Add rice; cover and simmer until rice is tender, about 20 minutes.
2. Beat eggs until frothy in a bowl; add lemon juice. Beat in 2 cups of broth very slowly; stir the mixture into the remaining soup.
3. Heat to serving temperature, being very careful not to let it boil (boiling will curdle the egg).

4 to 6 servings

Suggested accompaniment: Pita (page 54).

Pita

Pita (alias Greek or Syrian Pocket Bread, or Bible Bread) is unusually versatile. It can be eaten plain or filled with a variety of sandwich fillings to be a meal in itself.

7½ to 8 cups all-purpose flour
2 packages active dry yeast
2 tablespoons sugar
2 teaspoons salt
2½ cups hot water (120°-130°F)
¼ cup olive or vegetable oil
1 cup cornmeal

1. Combine 2 cups flour, yeast, sugar, and salt in a large mixing bowl.
2. Stir in water and oil; beat until smooth.
3. Stir in enough remaining flour to make a soft dough.
4. Turn out onto a floured surface; continue to work in flour until dough is stiff enough to knead. Knead until smooth and elastic (about 5 minutes).
5. Place in an oiled bowl; turn to oil top of dough. Cover; let rise in a warm place until double in bulk (about 45 minutes).
6. Punch dough down and divide into 8 equal parts. Roll each into a ball. Let dough rest 5 minutes. Roll 4 of the balls into 8-inch rounds, ⅛ inch thick. Sprinkle 2 greased baking sheets with cornmeal. Place rounds on baking sheets. Cover; let rise 30 minutes. (See Note.)
7. Bake at 450°F 8 to 10 minutes, or until puffed and brown. Prepare the 4 remaining loaves in the same manner.

Eight 8-inch loaves

Note: Be careful when handling the dough not to crease or pinch it, or the pockets won't form.

Chicken Soup Tortellini

2 quarts water
1 broiler-fryer chicken (about 2½ pounds)
1 onion, sliced
2 teaspoons fresh minced parsley or 1 teaspoon dried parsley
1½ teaspoons salt
1 teaspoon rosemary or chervil
⅛ teaspoon pepper
1 cup sliced celery with leaves
1 cup sliced fresh mushrooms
½ cup dry white wine
32 tortellini (see recipe)

1. Place water, chicken, onion, parsley, salt, rosemary, and pepper in a large saucepan. Bring to boiling; simmer covered 1 hour, or until chicken is tender.
2. Remove chicken; cool. Discard chicken skin. Remove meat from bones and chop fine. Reserve for tortellini filling.
3. Bring stock to boiling; stir in remaining ingredients. Simmer 15 minutes, or until tortellini are done. (If using frozen tortellini, simmer about 30 minutes.)

8 to 10 servings

Suggested accompaniment: Crispy Breadsticks.

Tortellini

Dough:
2 eggs
2 egg whites
2 tablespoons olive or vegetable oil
2 teaspoons salt
3 cups all-purpose flour
Filling:
2½ cups finely chopped chicken

1. Prepare dough by combining eggs, egg whites, oil, and salt in a bowl. Gradually add flour, mixing well until mixture forms a soft dough. Turn onto a floured surface and knead in remaining flour to form a very stiff dough.
2. Wrap dough in waxed paper; let rest 10 minutes.
3. Combine chicken, cheese, and egg yolks in a bowl. Set aside.
4. Divide dough in quarters. Roll each quarter into a large circle as thin as possible. Cut into about 32 (2-inch) rounds.

¼ cup grated Parmesan cheese
2 egg yolks

5. For each tortellini, place about 1 teaspoon chicken mixture in center of round. Moisten edges with water. Fold in half; seal edges. Shape into rings by stretching the tips of half circle slightly and wrapping the ring around your index finger. Gently press tips together (tortellini may be frozen at this point).
6. Cook as directed in recipe for Chicken Soup Tortellini.

About 128 tortellini

Crispy Breadsticks

1 cup whole wheat flour
1 package active dry yeast
1 tablespoon sugar
1 teaspoon salt
⅔ cup hot water
2 tablespoons vegetable oil
1 to 1¼ cups all-purpose flour

1. Stir together whole wheat flour, yeast, sugar, and salt in a mixing bowl.
2. Blend in water and oil; beat until smooth.
3. Stir in enough flour to form a soft dough.
4. Turn onto a floured surface; continue to work in flour until dough is stiff enough to knead. Knead until smooth and elastic (about 5 minutes), working in as much flour as possible. (The more flour, the crispier the bread sticks.)
5. Cover with bowl; let rest about 30 minutes.
6. Divide dough in quarters. Divide each quarter into 8 equal pieces. For ease in shaping, allow dough to rest about 10 minutes. Roll each piece with palms of hands into 10-inch lengths.
7. Place on greased baking sheets about ½ inch apart. If desired, brush with a mixture of 1 egg white and 1 teaspoon water.
8. Bake at 325°F 20 minutes, or until golden brown and crispy.

32 bread sticks

French Onion Soup *(Soupe à l'Oignon)*

The originator of this famous French soup was King Louis XV, who returned late one night to his hunting lodge and found only onions, butter, and champagne on hand. So hungry and weary was he that he simply mixed them together. Voilà—French Onion Soup! A toasted cheese crouton is traditionally part of the recipe, so there's no need to serve additional bread.

5 medium onions, sliced (4 cups)
3 tablespoons butter or margarine
1½ quarts beef broth
½ teaspoon salt
⅛ teaspoon pepper
Cheese Croutons

1. Sauté onions in melted butter in a large saucepan. Cook slowly, stirring until golden (about 10 minutes).
2. Blend in beef broth, salt, and pepper. Bring to boiling, cover, and simmer 15 minutes.
3. Pour soup into warm soup bowls or crocks. Float a cheese crouton in each bowl of soup.

6 servings

Cheese Croutons

6 slices French bread, toasted
2 tablespoons butter or margarine
¼ cup (1 ounce) grated Gruyère or
   Swiss cheese

1. Spread one side of each bread slice with butter. If necessary, cut bread to fit size of bowl. Sprinkle cheese over buttered toast.
2. Place under broiler until cheese melts.

Hungarian Goulash Soup

The Hungarians use grated potato for a thickening in this soup, with wonderful results.

1½ pounds beef for stew, cut into ½-inch cubes
1 tablespoon shortening or vegetable oil
1 large onion, chopped
1 quart water
¾ cup grated potato (about 1 large)
1 tablespoon paprika
1 tablespoon tomato sauce or ketchup
1 teaspoon salt
½ teaspoon caraway seed (optional)
¼ teaspoon crushed thyme
Pinch red pepper
1 cup chopped pared raw potato (about 1 large)
1 cup uncooked egg noodles

1. Brown meat in shortening in a large saucepan. Add onion; cook until tender.
2. Add water, grated potato, and seasonings. Bring to boiling; cover. Simmer 1½ hours, or until beef is tender.
3. Stir in potatoes and noodles. Cook until tender, 10 to 20 minutes.

4 to 6 servings

Suggested accompaniment: Peasant Black Bread.

Hungarian Goulash Soup with Spaetzle: Follow recipe for Hungarian Goulash Soup, omitting chopped potato and noodles. Serve with **hot buttered spaetzle.**

Spaetzle

2 cups all-purpose flour
1 teaspoon salt
1 egg
¼ to ½ cup water

1. Combine flour and salt; stir in egg. Gradually add water until batter is stiff, but smooth. Place on wet cutting board; flatten.
2. With a wet knife, scrape small pieces of dough off and drop into boiling salted water. Cook only one layer of spaetzle at a time, boiling gently 5 to 8 minutes, or until done. Remove with perforated spoon.

Note: Spaetzle may be served in pea, lentil, or tomato soup or as a side dish, either tossed with hot melted butter or sautéed in butter. For variety, sprinkle with toasted bread crumbs or grated Parmesan cheese.

Peasant Black Bread

3½ cups rye flour
½ cup unsweetened cocoa
¼ cup sugar
3 tablespoons caraway seed
2 packages active dry yeast
1 tablespoon instant coffee (powder or crystals)
2 teaspoons salt
2½ cups hot water (120°-130°F)
¼ cup vinegar
¼ cup dark molasses
¼ cup vegetable oil or melted butter
3½ to 4½ cups unbleached or all-purpose flour

1. Thoroughly mix rye flour, cocoa, sugar, caraway, yeast, coffee, and salt in a large mixing bowl.
2. Stir in water, vinegar, molasses, and oil; beat until smooth.
3. Stir in enough unbleached flour to make a soft dough.
4. Turn onto a floured surface. Knead until smooth and elastic (about 5 minutes).
5. Place in an oiled bowl; turn to oil top of dough. Cover; let rise in warm place until doubled (about 1 hour).
6. Punch dough down. Divide in half; shape each half into a ball and place in center of 2 greased 8-inch round cake pans. Cover; let rise until double in bulk (about 1 hour).
7. Bake at 350°F 40 to 45 minutes, or until done.

2 loaves

Mulligatawny Soup

Mulligatawny soup is from India, and as you might expect, the distinctive flavor is curry. Curry recipes do not always call for curry powder. The authentic ones call for a combination of spices, such as turmeric, cumin, coriander, dill, and cardamom. This version of mulligatawny calls for both curry powder and several other seasonings.

1 cup diced uncooked chicken (see Note)
¼ cup chopped onion
¼ cup chopped celery
¼ cup diced carrot
2 tart apples, pared and sliced
¼ cup fat or margarine
¼ cup flour
1 teaspoon curry powder
1½ quarts chicken broth
1 tomato, peeled and chopped, or 1 cup drained canned tomatoes, chopped
½ green pepper, minced
1 teaspoon minced parsley
1 teaspoon salt
1 teaspoon sugar
⅛ teaspoon pepper
⅛ teaspoon mace
2 whole cloves
1 cup cooked rice (optional)

1. Cook chicken, onion, celery, carrots, and apple in melted fat in a large saucepan until lightly browned.
2. Stir in flour and curry powder. Gradually add chicken broth, stirring constantly.
3. Stir in remaining ingredients. Cook, covered, over low heat until chicken is tender.
4. Remove and reserve chicken. Strain soup, discarding cloves.
5. Purée vegetables in an electric blender or force through a sieve or food mill. Return soup and vegetable purée to saucepan. Mix in chicken and heat to serving temperature.
6. If desired, mix in hot cooked rice.

8 servings

Suggested accompaniment: Indian Flat Bread.

Note: If making your own chicken broth, substitute the cooked chicken meat for the uncooked chicken and add to soup for final heating.

Indian Flat Bread (Nan)

From the northwest region of India comes Indian Flat Bread, baked at a high temperature in clay ovens. This is a richer, more sophisticated bread than the unleavened chapati eaten by most Indians. Both breads are literally the staff of life.

1 cup all-purpose flour
1 package active dry yeast
2 teaspoons salt
1 cup hot water (120°-130°F)
¼ cup buttermilk or yogurt
1 egg (at room temperature)
2 tablespoons vegetable oil
1 tablespoon honey or sugar
2 to 3 cups all-purpose flour
Melted butter (optional)
Cornmeal or sesame or poppy seeds (optional)

1. Combine 1 cup flour, yeast, and salt in a mixing bowl.
2. Stir in water, buttermilk, egg, oil, and honey; beat until smooth.
3. Stir in enough remaining flour to form a soft, sticky dough.
4. Turn onto a floured surface; continue to work in flour until dough is stiff enough to knead. Knead until smooth and elastic, but still soft (3 to 5 minutes).
5. Place in an oiled bowl; turning once to oil top of dough. Cover; let rise until double in bulk (about 45 minutes).
6. Punch dough down. Shape into 16 equal balls. Let rest 5 minutes. Roll out each ball to a ¼-inch-thick round. If desired, brush with melted butter and sprinkle with cornmeal, sesame, or poppy seeds. Set on baking sheets.
7. Bake at 450°F 5 to 8 minutes.

16 round loaves

LUNCH BOX SPECIALS

More and more meals are being eaten away from home today. That means people are either eating lunch in a restaurant or carrying it from home.

The lunch-box carriers have a lot of choice in the variety of shapes and sizes of containers they use. That makes it possible to carry almost anything hot or cold from home. Thermoses are now designed both with the traditional opening for liquids or wide-mouth openings for transporting chunky foods, including soups.

Selected in this section are soups and breads that both kids and adults will enjoy having tucked into the lunch box. Or you may choose from the other recipes in this book to pack some excitement into that lunch box for yourself, a child, a husband, or friend.

Tomato-Cheese Soup

1 can (about 10 ounces) condensed tomato soup
1 soup can milk
1 cup (4 ounces) shredded Cheddar, American, or Colby cheese
¼ teaspoon finely crushed basil (optional)

1. Turn soup into a large saucepan; gradually blend in milk. Stir until hot and blended.
2. Mix in cheese and, if desired, basil.

3 servings

Suggested accompaniment: Pocket Bread with desired filling.

Pocket Bread

2 cups all-purpose flour
2 packages active dry yeast
2 tablespoons sugar or honey
2 teaspoons salt
2½ cups hot water (120°-130°F)
¼ cup vegetable oil
5½ to 6 cups all-purpose flour

1. Combine 2 cups flour, yeast, sugar, and salt in a large mixing bowl.
2. Stir in water and oil; beat until smooth.
3. Stir in enough remaining flour to make a soft dough.
4. Turn onto a floured surface; continue to work in flour until stiff enough to knead. Knead until smooth and elastic (about 5 minutes).
5. Place in an oiled bowl; turn to oil top of dough. Cover; let rise in a warm place until double in bulk (about 45 minutes).
6. Punch dough down. Divide in half. Divide each half into 10 equal pieces. Roll each piece into a ball. Let dough rest 5 minutes. Roll balls into 3- or 4-inch rounds, ⅛ inch thick. Place on greased baking sheets. Cover; let rise 30 minutes (see Note).
7. Bake at 450°F 5 to 8 minutes, or until puffed and brown.

20 pocket breads

Note: Avoid pinching or creasing dough after rolling, or bread will not puff properly.

Alphabet Soup

½ pound ground beef
1 onion, chopped
5 cups water
1 can (16 ounces) tomatoes
3 potatoes, cubed
2 carrots, sliced
2 stalks celery, sliced
2 teaspoons salt
1 teaspoon Worcestershire sauce
1 beef bouillon cube
¼ teaspoon garlic powder
¼ teaspoon pepper
3 sprigs fresh parsley, minced, or 2 tablespoons dried
1 cup uncooked alphabet macaroni

1. Brown meat in a large saucepan; drain off fat.
2. Add remaining ingredients, except macaroni. Bring to boiling; cover and simmer 1 hour.
3. Stir in macaroni; cook 20 minutes.

6 to 8 servings

Suggested accompaniment: banana bread-cream cheese sandwiches (see Grandma Louise's Banana Loaf).

Grandma Louise's Banana Loaf

1 cup sugar
½ cup shortening
1 cup mashed fully ripe bananas (2 to 3 bananas)
1 egg
¼ cup buttermilk
1¾ cups all-purpose flour
1½ teaspoons baking powder
1 teaspoon baking soda
½ teaspoon salt

1. Combine sugar, shortening, bananas, egg, and buttermilk in a mixing bowl; beat well.
2. Blend remaining ingredients, add to banana mixture, and mix until blended (about 1 minute).
3. Turn into a greased 9×5×3-inch loaf pan.
4. Bake at 350°F 45 to 50 minutes, or until done.

1 loaf

Homemade Chicken-Noodle Soup

2 quarts water
1 broiler-fryer chicken (about 2½ pounds), cut up
1 finely chopped onion
1 cup finely chopped celery
2 tablespoons minced fresh parsley or 1 teaspoon dried
2 teaspoons salt
1 teaspoon crushed rosemary or chervil
⅛ teaspoon pepper
2 cups uncooked homemade (see page 60) or packaged noodles

1. Place all ingredients except noodles in a kettle or Dutch oven. Bring to boiling; simmer 1 hour, or until chicken is tender.
2. Remove chicken; cool. Discard skin. Remove meat from bones and chop.
3. Return chicken to stock; bring to boiling. Stir in noodles. Simmer 20 to 30 minutes, or until noodles are done.

8 servings

Suggested accompaniment: New England Blueberry Muffins (page 60).

Homemade Noodles

2 eggs
½ teaspoon salt
1 cup all-purpose flour

1. Beat eggs and salt in a mixing bowl. Gradually add flour, mixing well until mixture forms a soft dough. Turn onto a floured surface; knead in remaining flour to form a very stiff dough.
2. Cover; let rest 10 to 15 minutes.
3. Roll dough as thin as possible, turning dough over as you roll.
4. Roll dough up tightly, jelly-roll fashion. Cut off thin slices. Toss to separate. Spread out on baking sheets; toss periodically until thoroughly dry.

2 cups noodles

New England Blueberry Muffins

In New England, they fill the muffin cups right up to the top with batter to produce these giant round-top muffins. If you like yours more petite, fill the muffin cups ⅔ full and reduce baking time by 5 minutes.

1 cup sugar
½ cup softened butter or margarine
2 eggs
½ cup milk
2 cups all-purpose flour
2 teaspoons baking powder
½ teaspoon salt
1 to 1½ cups fresh or frozen
    blueberries

1. Combine sugar, butter, eggs, and milk in a mixing bowl; beat well.
2. Blend flour, baking powder, and salt; add and mix until blended (about 1 minute). Fold in blueberries.
3. Spoon into 12 well-greased muffin cups, filling almost to the top of the cup.
4. Bake at 375°F 20 to 25 minutes.

12 large muffins

Hot Dog! It's Soup

One way of improving your child's acceptance of food is to allow him or her to have a hand in its preparation. With this soup we are mixing two favorite children's foods—corn and hot dogs. You might ask your child to help you shred the cheese (under your supervision, of course) or slice the hot dogs (a table knife will do). Serve with buttered slices of homemade white bread. That's one of their favorites, too.

½ cup chopped onion
⅓ cup sliced celery
2 tablespoons margarine
1 cup water
2 cups (16-ounce can) cream-style
    corn
1 bay leaf
½ teaspoon basil
1½ cups milk
1 pound frankfurters, sliced
1 teaspoon salt
⅛ teaspoon pepper
½ cup shredded process American
    cheese
    Minced parsley

1. Sauté onion and celery in margarine in a medium saucepan. Add water, corn, bay leaf, and basil. Cook 5 minutes.
2. Remove bay leaf. Add remaining ingredients except parsley. Cook over low heat until cheese melts.
3. Garnish with parsley.

6 to 8 servings

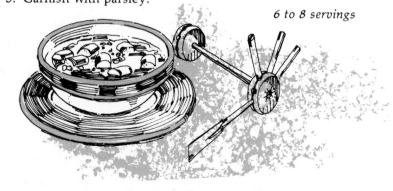

SOUP

The humble stockpot has been around since pre-recorded history. During the Middle Ages, European words emerged resembling the sound made when one sipped soup. Thus, the word "soup" and its cousins soop, soupe, zup, and soep came into the language. In France, soup was served so often at the evening meal that the meal became known as *souper*, or supper.

The first soups were made from whatever foods were available at the time, like bones, meat, and wild roots. Today, with all the advancements of modern civilization, soup is still being prepared by the very same simple methods.

Soups are based on flavorful stocks made from simmering fish, meat, bones, vegetables, and seasonings in water for a long period of time. The broth is strained and various fresh ingredients are added to make the soup. This is truly the place where you can use your imagination and add "everything but the kitchen sink" to make a flavorful soup brimming with nourishment.

Adaptability is soup's middle name. Soup can be made days ahead and reheated to be served with a salad or cheese and bread for a delightfully easy dinner. Or it can be the elegant opener at a formal dinner party. Remember, sometimes the most gourmet-sounding and -tasting soups are the easiest to prepare.

To vary the texture and flavor of your soups, try puréeing the cooked vegetables with about one cup of the stock in an electric blender or foodmill.

On rush days, a few quick additions such as pasta, fresh, frozen, or canned vegetables, or chopped leftover meats to a simple broth will give you a quick, sumptuous, and best of all . . . homemade soup.

STOCKING UP

There are several different types of stocks used to produce various flavorful soups. White stock is a broth with no color and is made with poultry or veal and vegetables. Brown stock is made with beef and vegetables that are first browned. Vegetable stock is made with carrots, onions, celery, and bones and trimmings and herbs. All stocks are simmered slowly 1 to 2 hours and use approximately 1 cup of meat, bones, and vegetables to 2 cups water.

Stock-making is economical because food scraps that otherwise might be discarded can be used. Well-scrubbed vegetable peelings are excellent flavoring agents and nutritious, since most of the vitamins and minerals are located just under the skin.

Other items you might not have recognized as being good stock ingredients are carrot and celery tops, turkey carcasses, chicken necks and giblets, and bones of all sorts. These items can be collected gradually and kept in a plastic bag in the freezer. When the bag is full, it's time to make some stock.

Herbs play an important part in making the stock distinctive. They may be added in the beginning when you add the vegetables, or, if you prefer a more subtle herb flavor, toward the end of the cooking time, and simmered about 30 minutes.

Cooked bones and fresh bones each impart their own special flavor to stock. However, it is best not to combine them in the same stock because they tend to make it cloudy when used together. To add a superb flavor to stocks, add bone marrow. People have even been known to crack or crush the bones to get out the flavor.

Some meats contain quite a bit of fat which will make the stock too greasy. If the soup will be served immediately, the fat should be skimmed off the top. If you have the time, the easiest way to remove the fat is to chill the stock. The fat then rises to the top and forms a protective covering. When you are ready to use it, scrape off the fat layer before heating.

Stock may be stored in a covered container in the refrigerator for a few days or in the freezer for a few months. Freeze it in one or two-cup portions for easier use in recipes, if desired. For quick identification, label the stock with its name and date of entry into the freezer.

Brown Vegetable Stock

Use assorted vegetables from your refrigerator, or purchase a package of soup vegetables from your produce counter.

    **2 pounds mixed vegetables
       (carrots, leeks, onions, celery,
       turnips, etc.)
  ¼ cup butter or margarine
2½ quarts water
  ½ teaspoon salt
  ½ teaspoon thyme
  3 sprigs parsley
  ½ bay leaf
    Dash of pepper**

1. Chop vegetables. Brown in butter.
2. Add water and seasonings. Cover.
3. Simmer 1½ hours or until vegetables are tender.
4. Strain and chill.

About 2 quarts stock

White Vegetable Stock:
If a lighter, clearer stock is desired, omit butter and do not brown vegetables.

Beef Stock

Because during simmering the liquid is reduced, salt lightly initially and correct salt level before serving.

  **3 pounds lean beef (chuck or plate),
    cut in 1-inch pieces
  1 soup bone, cracked
  3 quarts cold water
  1 tablespoon salt
  2 large onions, peeled
  2 whole cloves
  5 carrots, cut in large pieces
  3 stalks celery with leaves, sliced
  4 sprigs parsley
  1 bay leaf
  1 teaspoon thyme
  8 peppercorns**

1. Put meat and soup bone into a large saucepan; add water and salt. Cover saucepan and simmer about 2 hours, removing foam as necessary.
2. Slice 1 onion; insert the cloves into second onion. Add onions, remaining vegetables, and seasonings to saucepan. Cover and bring to boiling. Reduce heat and simmer about 1½ hours.
3. Remove from heat; remove soup bone and strain stock through a fine sieve. Allow to cool. Chill. (The meat and vegetables strained from stock may be served as desired.)
4. Remove fat that rises to surface (reserve for use in other food preparation). Reheat and serve with slices of crisp toast.

About 2½ quarts stock

Brown Stock:
Follow recipe for Beef Stock. Cut meat from soup bone and brown it along with beef pieces in ¼ **cup fat** in saucepan before cooking. Proceed as in Beef Stock.

White Stock:
Follow recipe for Beef Stock. Substitute

veal shank and breast or a disjointed stewing chicken for beef.

Consommé: Follow recipe for White Stock. Cool stock and stir in 2 egg whites, slightly beaten, crushed shells of eggs, and 1 ice cube if further cooling is needed. Heat slowly to boiling, stirring constantly. Remove from heat and let stand 25 minutes. Strain through a double thickness of cheesecloth.

HEARTY MAIN DISH SOUPS

Americans are ingenious in their ways of adapting recipes from all over the world. The "great melting pot" approach with soups gives us hearty, wholesome meals. Different parts of the country have certain foods indigenous to that area. New England, for instance, is famous for its chowders; the Gulf region for its gumbos; the Shaker or potato belt for potato soups; the West for its chili. They all offer soups with individual flair.

For a satisfying meal that is easy to prepare, couple some of the hot, hearty soups included here with bread and salad.

Baked Minestrone

1½ pounds lean beef for stew, cut
    in 1-inch cubes
 1 cup coarsely chopped onion
 2 cloves garlic, crushed
 1 teaspoon salt
¼ teaspoon pepper
 2 tablespoons olive oil
 3 cans (about 10 ounces each)
    condensed beef broth
 2 soup cans water
1½ teaspoons herb seasoning
 1 can (16 ounces) tomatoes
    (undrained)
 1 can (15¼ ounces) kidney beans
    (undrained)
 1 can (6 ounces) pitted ripe olives
    (undrained)
1½ cups thinly sliced carrots
 1 cup small seashell macaroni
 2 cups sliced zucchini
    Grated Parmesan cheese

1. Mix beef, onion, garlic, salt, and pepper in a large saucepan. Add olive oil and stir to coat meat evenly.
2. Bake at 400°F 30 minutes, or until meat is browned, stirring occasionally.
3. Turn oven control to 350°F. Add broth, water, and seasonings; stir. Cover; cook 1 hour, or until meat is tender.
4. Stir in tomatoes, kidney beans, olives, carrots, and macaroni. Put sliced zucchini on top. Cover; bake 30 to 40 minutes, or until carrots are tender.
5. Serve with grated cheese.

10 to 12 servings

Suggested accompaniment: Mozzarella Egg Bread (page 19).

Red and White Bean Soup

There are many dried white beans on the market—great northern, navy, white, kidney, and lima are some. They may be used interchangeably and are all high in protein.

2 cups dried navy beans, soaked overnight
2 cups chopped onion
1 tablespoon salt
10 whole peppercorns
1 stalk celery with leaves, sliced
¼ cup minced parsley or 2 tablespoons dried parsley
½ teaspoon crushed thyme or basil
2 cups chopped potato
¼ cup butter or margarine
¼ cup flour
1 can (15 ounces) tomato sauce
1 can (14 ounces) brown beans in molasses sauce

1. Drain soaked beans, reserving liquid. Add enough water to bean liquid to measure 6 cups. Combine in a large saucepan soaked beans, bean liquid, onion, salt, peppercorns, celery, parsley, and thyme. Heat to boiling; simmer 45 minutes.
2. Stir in potato. Simmer 20 minutes or until tender.
3. In a separate saucepan, stir flour into melted butter; cook until bubbly. Gradually add tomato sauce; mix well.
4. Stir tomato mixture and brown beans into soup. Simmer 5 minutes.

8 servings

Suggested accompaniment: Triple Treat Bread (page 22).

Chili Soup

½ pound ground beef
1 cup chopped onion
5 cups water
1 can (28 ounces) tomatoes
1 can (15 ounces) tomato sauce
1 clove garlic, crushed
1 tablespoon chili powder
1 teaspoon salt
1 teaspoon cumin
½ teaspoon oregano
1 cup uncooked macaroni
1 can (about 15 ounces) kidney or chili beans

1. Brown meat in a large saucepan; drain off fat. Stir in onion; cook 1 minute.
2. Add water, tomatoes, tomato sauce, garlic, chili powder, salt, cumin, and oregano. Simmer 30 minutes.
3. Add remaining ingredients; cook until macaroni is done (about 10 to 15 minutes).

8 to 10 servings

Suggested accompaniment: Sunshine Corn Muffins (page 46).

Yellow Pea Soup

2 cups dried yellow split peas
1 pound smoked shoulder roll or meaty ham bone
7 cups water
1 cup chopped onion
1 teaspoon salt
½ teaspoon sugar
1 teaspoon crushed thyme
¼ cup butter or margarine
¼ cup flour
2 cups milk

1. Combine peas, meat, water, onion, salt, sugar, and thyme in a large saucepan. Bring to boiling; simmer 1½ to 2 hours.
2. Remove meat; skim fat from soup.
3. Stir flour into melted butter in a saucepan; cook until bubbly. Gradually add milk, stirring constantly. Bring to boiling; cook 1 minute.
4. Stir white sauce into soup. Serve with thin slices of the meat.

6 to 8 servings

Suggested accompaniment: small Kaiser Rolls (page 27).

Beef Barley Soup, 70;
Cornmeal French Bread, 21

Bean and Prosciutto Soup

2 cups (about ¾ pound) dried beans, soaked overnight
5 cups water
2 cups sliced celery
3 to 4 ounces sliced prosciutto, cut in thin strips
1 can (16 ounces) tomatoes
1 can (about 10 ounces) condensed beef broth
1 teaspoon salt
1 garlic clove, crushed
2 packages (9 ounces each) frozen Italian green beans
3 sprigs fresh parsley, minced (about 2 tablespoons)

1. Combine soaked dried beans, water, celery, prosciutto, tomatoes, beef broth, salt, and garlic in a 5-quart saucepot. Bring to boiling; simmer, covered, 30 minutes.
2. Mix in green beans and parsley; simmer 5 to 10 minutes.

10 to 12 servings

Suggested accompaniment: Crusty Hard Rolls (page 27).

Tomato-Lentil Soup

2 cups chopped carrots
1 cup chopped onion
1 cup sliced celery
2 tablespoons margarine, melted
1 clove garlic, crushed
1¼ cups (½ pound) dried lentils
2 quarts water
1 tablespoon salt
1 can (6 ounces) tomato paste
¼ teaspoon crushed dill weed or tarragon

1. Sauté carrots, onion, and celery in margarine in a large saucepan until tender.
2. Add garlic, lentils, water, and salt. Simmer 2 hours, or until lentils are tender.
3. Add tomato paste and dill weed; stir.

6 to 8 servings

Suggested accompaniment: Sweet and Sourdough Granola Bread (page 39).

Split Pea Soup with Ham Bone

2 cups dried green split peas
1½ quarts water
1 ham bone (about 1½ pounds)
1 onion, sliced
1 cup sliced celery
1 cup grated carrot
2 teaspoons salt
1 teaspoon crushed basil
¼ cup butter or margarine
¼ cup flour
2 cups milk

1. In a large saucepan, combine peas, water, bone, onion, celery, carrot, salt, and basil. Bring to boiling; simmer 1½ to 2 hours.
2. Stir flour into melted butter in a separate saucepan; cook until bubbly. Gradually add milk, stirring constantly. Bring to boiling; cook 1 minute.
3. Stir white sauce into soup.

8 servings

Suggested accompaniment: Anadama Batter Bread (page 24).

Creamy Cheddar Cheese Soup, 75;
Vegetable Oyster Soup, 73

Lentil Soup

1¼ cups (about ½ pound) lentils,
    soaked overnight
2 quarts beef broth
6 frankfurters, cut diagonally in
    ½-inch slices
2 onions, thinly sliced
2 carrots, sliced
2 stalks celery, sliced
3 sprigs chervil or parsley or 1
    tablespoon dried chervil
2 teaspoons salt
¼ teaspoon pepper

Combine all ingredients in a large saucepan. Bring to boiling; simmer 35 minutes, or until lentils are tender.

8 servings

Suggested accompaniment: Bran-New Batter Bread (page 25).

Chicken Succotash Soup with Parsley Dumplings

1 broiler-fryer chicken (2 to 3
    pounds), cut up
2 quarts water
2 teaspoons salt
½ teaspoon crushed rosemary
    Pinch pepper
    Parsley Dumplings
1 cup sliced carrots
¼ cup chopped onion
1 package (10 ounces) frozen corn
1 package (10 ounces) frozen lima
    beans

1. Combine chicken, water, salt, rosemary, and pepper in a large saucepan. Bring to boiling; simmer 45 minutes, covered, or until chicken is tender.
2. Remove chicken from broth; cool, skin, and cut into pieces.
3. Skim fat or chill to remove fat (see page 62).
4. Prepare Parsley Dumplings.
5. Add vegetables and chicken to stock. Bring to boiling. Drop dumplings by teaspoonfuls onto gently simmering soup. Cover; cook 10 minutes. Uncover; cook 5 to 10 minutes.
6. Serve each portion with one or two dumplings.

6 to 8 servings

Parsley Dumplings

2 cups all-purpose flour
2 teaspoons baking powder
1½ teaspoons salt
⅛ teaspoon pepper
3 tablespoons butter or margarine
1 egg
    Milk
¼ cup minced parsley

1. Combine flour, baking powder, salt, and pepper in a bowl.
2. Cut in butter until mixture resembles coarse meal.
3. Break egg into measuring cup. Add enough milk to make 1 cup liquid. Beat well. Add to dry ingredients along with parsley and stir just until flour is moistened.
4. Proceed as directed.

Lebanon Lentil Soup

2 quarts beef broth
1 ham bone
1¼ cups (about ½ pound) lentils
2 stalks celery, sliced
2 carrots, sliced
1 onion, sliced
1 teaspoon salt
¼ teaspoon pepper
½ teaspoon crushed thyme or ¼
    teaspoon dill weed

1. Combine all ingredients in a large saucepan. Bring to boiling. Cover; simmer 1 to 2 hours, or until lentils are tender.
2. Remove ham bone. Force soup mixture through a coarse sieve or food mill, or purée in an electric blender.
3. Heat, if necessary.

8 servings

Suggested accompaniment: Pocket Bread (page 58).

Cream of Lentil Soup: Follow recipe for Lebanon Lentil Soup. After puréeing, stir in **1 cup half-and-half** or **whipping cream.**

Italian White Bean Soup

2 cups (about ½ pound) dried navy
    beans, soaked overnight
2 quarts water
2 cups chopped potato (about 1
    large)
1 can (16 ounces) tomatoes
    (undrained)
¼ cup chopped onion
2 teaspoons salt
1 clove garlic, crushed
1 teaspoon crushed basil
1 cup (about 2 ounces) broken
    vermicelli or shell macaroni

1. Combine in a large saucepan beans, water, potato, tomatoes, onion, salt, garlic, and basil. Bring to boiling; simmer 1 hour, or until beans are tender.
2. Stir in vermicelli; cook 20 minutes.

8 to 10 servings

Suggested accompaniment: Quick Strips (page 50).

Lancaster County Chicken-Corn Soup

The "rivvels" served in this soup are a Pennsylvania Dutch dumpling made by rubbing bits of the dough mixture between the palms of your hands and dropping them into the soup.

1 stewing chicken (3 to 4 pounds),
    cut up
1 large onion, chopped
3 quarts water
2 teaspoons salt
¼ teaspoon pepper
4 cups corn (three 10-ounce
    packages frozen corn or two
    16-ounce cans)
½ cup chopped celery with leaves
    Rivvels

1. Place chicken, onion, water, salt, and pepper in a large saucepot. Bring to boiling; simmer 1 hour or until chicken is tender.
2. Remove chicken from stock, strip meat from bones, cut into bite-size pieces, and return to stock. Add corn and celery; simmer 30 minutes.
3. Drop rivvels into soup by rivveling; that is, rubbing dough between palms of your hands and dropping into soup. Cook in simmering soup 15 minutes, or until done.

10 servings

Suggested accompaniment: Pan Rolls (page 26).

Rivvels: Combine 1 cup all-purpose flour, **½ teaspoon salt, 1 egg,** and enough **milk (about ¼ cup)** to make a crumbly semimoist mixture.

Chili-Chicken Soup

1 broiler-fryer chicken (about 3 pounds), cut up
1½ quarts water
1 onion, studded with 2 or 3 whole cloves
1 tablespoon salt
3 garlic cloves, crushed
1 bay leaf
1 can (about 15 ounces) red kidney beans
1 can (6 ounces) tomato paste
1 can (4 ounces) mild green chilies or 1 hot pepper, chopped
1 tablespoon chili powder
1 teaspoon crushed basil
Cooked rice

1. Combine chicken, water, onion, salt, garlic, and bay leaf in a large saucepan. Bring to boiling; simmer 45 minutes, or until chicken is tender.
2. Remove chicken and onion from stock; cool. Discard chicken skin; remove meat from bones and chop. Skim fat from stock (see page 62). Remove cloves from onion; discard. Chop onion.
3. Stir chicken, onion, and remaining ingredients, except rice, into stock. Heat. Serve with rice.

6 to 8 servings

Suggested accompaniment: Quick Strips (page 50).

Burgundy Oxtail Soup

2 oxtails (about 3 pounds), cut up
¼ cup flour (about)
3 tablespoons bacon fat or shortening
2 quarts water
1 onion, chopped
¾ cup tomato juice
2 teaspoons salt
1 bay leaf
4 peppercorns
1 garlic clove, crushed
1 cup sliced celery with leaves
1 cup sliced carrot
¾ cup burgundy or other dry red wine
½ teaspoon crushed tarragon
1 cup sliced fresh mushrooms
¼ cup chopped fresh parsley

1. Coat oxtails with flour. Brown in hot fat in a large saucepan.
2. Add water, onion, tomato juice, salt, bay leaf, peppercorns, and garlic. Bring to boiling; simmer 2 to 3 hours.
3. Strain stock. Chill; remove fat. Return stock to saucepan.
4. Bring stock to boiling; add celery, carrot, burgundy, and tarragon. Simmer 30 minutes.
5. Stir in remaining ingredients. Cook 5 minutes.

8 servings

Suggested accompaniment: Biscuits (page 44).

Belgian Beer Soup

Soups provide great ways to cook less-tender cuts of meat. Most of these meats are flavorful and relatively inexpensive, and best of all they become tender through long, slow simmering.

2 pounds beef chuck, cut in ½-inch cubes; reserve bone
7 cups water
1 cup beer
2 teaspoons salt
1 bay leaf

1. Trim fat from meat.
2. Brown meat and bone in a large saucepan without fat. Stir in water, beer, salt, bay leaf, pepper, allspice, and bouillon cubes. Heat to boiling; simmer 2 hours.
3. Stir in onion, potatoes, celery, and carrots; simmer 30 minutes.

½ teaspoon pepper
½ teaspoon allspice
2 beef bouillon cubes
½ cup chopped onion
4 cups chopped potatoes (about 6 medium potatoes)
2 cups sliced celery
2 cups sliced carrots
1 package (10 ounces) frozen Brussels sprouts

4. Stir in Brussels sprouts; simmer 15 minutes, or until sprouts are tender.

6 to 8 servings

Suggested accompaniment: Hearty Potato Bread (page 20).

Sherried Chicken Chowder

10 cups water
1 broiler-fryer chicken (about 2½ pounds)
1 carrot, coarsely chopped
1 stalk celery, coarsely chopped
1 onion, halved
4 whole cloves
2 teaspoons salt
1 teaspoon crushed tarragon
1 bay leaf
½ cup uncooked barley or rice
½ teaspoon curry powder
¼ cup dry sherry
1 cup half-and-half

1. Place water, chicken, carrot, celery, onion halves studded with cloves, salt, and tarragon in Dutch oven or saucepot. Bring to boiling; simmer 1 hour, or until chicken is tender.
2. Remove chicken; cool. Discard skin; remove meat from bones; chop.
3. Strain stock. Discard cloves and bay leaf. Reserve stock and vegetables. Skim fat from stock (see page 62).
4. Purée vegetables and 1 cup stock in an electric blender.
5. Return stock to Dutch oven; bring to boiling. Stir in barley and puréed vegetables. Simmer 1 hour, or until barley is tender. Stir in chicken, curry, sherry, and half-and-half.

8 servings

Suggested accompaniment: Better Batter Rolls (page 30).

Meatball Soup

1 pound ground beef
1 onion, chopped
1½ quarts water
1 can (16 ounces) tomatoes
3 potatoes, cubed
2 carrots, sliced
2 stalks celery, sliced
3 sprigs fresh parsley, minced, or 2 tablespoons dried
½ cup uncooked barley
2 teaspoons salt
½ teaspoon crushed thyme or basil
¼ teaspoon garlic powder
¼ teaspoon pepper
1 bay leaf
1 teaspoon Worcestershire sauce
1 beef bouillon cube

1. Shape beef into tiny meatballs. Brown meatballs and onion in a large saucepan, or place in a shallow pan and brown in a 400°F oven. Drain off excess fat.
2. Add remaining ingredients. Bring to boiling, simmer 1½ hours, or until vegetables are tender.

8 servings

Suggested accompaniment: Braided Egg Bread (page 15).

Vegetable Medley Soup

8 slices bacon
½ cup chopped onion
½ cup sliced celery
5 cups water
1½ cups fresh corn or 1 package
    (about 10 ounces) frozen corn
½ cup sliced carrots
1 potato, pared and sliced
1 tablespoon salt
1 teaspoon sugar
¼ teaspoon pepper
¼ teaspoon crushed thyme or basil
1 cup fresh green beans, cut in
    1-inch pieces
4 cups chopped peeled tomatoes
    (4 to 5 tomatoes)

1. Cook bacon until crisp in a Dutch oven or kettle. Drain off all but 2 tablespoons fat.
2. Sauté onion and celery in bacon fat.
3. Stir in water, corn, carrots, potato, salt, sugar, pepper, and thyme. Bring to boiling; simmer covered 30 minutes.
4. Stir in green beans; simmer 10 minutes, or until beans are crisp-tender.
5. Stir in tomatoes; heat 5 minutes.

About 6 servings

Suggested accompaniment: Sourdough Sam's Skillet Loaves (page 39).

Vegetarian Chowder

4 cups sliced zucchini
½ cup chopped onion
⅓ cup butter or margarine
⅓ cup flour
2 tablespoons minced parsley
1 teaspoon crushed basil
1 teaspoon salt
⅛ teaspoon pepper
3 cups water
1 chicken bouillon cube
1 package (10 ounces) frozen corn
    or 2 cups fresh corn
1 can (13½ ounces) evaporated
    milk
1 can (16 ounces) tomatoes, broken
    up, or 3 tomatoes, skinned
    and chopped
1 cup shredded Monterey Jack
    cheese (optional)

1. Sauté zucchini and onion in butter in a large saucepan. Stir in flour, parsley, basil, salt, and pepper.
2. Gradually add water, stirring constantly. Add remaining ingredients. Bring to boiling; simmer 10 to 15 minutes.
3. If desired, stir in Monterey Jack cheese.

6 to 8 servings

Suggested accompaniment: Anadama Batter Bread (page 24).

Beef Barley Soup

2 quarts water
1 soup bone with meat
½ cup chopped celery tops
1 tablespoon salt
½ teaspoon pepper
½ cup uncooked regular barley

1. Combine water, bone, celery tops, salt, and pepper in a Dutch oven. Bring to boiling; cover tightly and simmer 1 to 2 hours.
2. Remove bone from stock; cool. Remove meat from bone; chop. Return to stock.
3. Stir in barley; continue cooking 30 minutes.

3 cups coarsely chopped cabbage
1 cup sliced carrots
1 cup sliced celery
2 cups sliced parsnips
2 cups thinly sliced onion
1 can (12 ounces) tomato paste

4. Add remaining ingredients; simmer 30 minutes, or until vegetables are tender.

8 to 10 servings

Suggested accompaniment: Cornmeal French Bread (page 21).

Cheddar-Corn Chowder

2½ cups water
1½ cups chopped potatoes
1 cup sliced carrots
½ cup sliced celery
¼ cup chopped onion or scallions
1½ teaspoons salt
¼ teaspoon pepper
¼ cup butter or margarine
¼ cup flour
2 cups milk
2½ cups shredded sharp Cheddar cheese (10 ounces)
1 can (16 ounces) cream-style corn or 2 cups fresh corn

1. Combine water, potatoes, carrots, celery, onion, salt, and pepper in a large saucepan. Cover; bring to boiling. Simmer 10 minutes, or until vegetables are tender.
2. Melt butter in a saucepan. Stir in flour; cook until bubbly. Gradually add milk, stirring constantly. Bring to boiling; cook 1 minute. Add cheese; stir until melted.
3. Gradually add cheese sauce to soup, stirring constantly. Stir in corn.

6 servings

Suggested accompaniment: Pumpkin Spice Rolls (page 28).

Vegetable-Beer Chowder

1 package (9 ounces) frozen green beans, thawed
1 package (10 ounces) frozen corn, thawed
¼ cup chopped onion
¼ cup butter or margarine
¼ cup flour
1 teaspoon salt
½ teaspoon dry mustard
2 cups milk
1 cup beer
2 cups shredded Cheddar cheese (8 ounces)

1. Sauté vegetables in melted butter in a large saucepan.
2. Stir in flour, salt, and dry mustard; cook until bubbly, stirring constantly.
3. Gradually add milk and beer, stirring constantly. Bring to boiling; cook 1 minute.
4. Stir in cheese until melted.

4 to 6 servings

Suggested accompaniment: Hurry-up Dinner Rolls (page 31).

LUNCHEON SOUPS

Soups can be as light and refreshing as a summer breeze. They don't all have to be served hot; they can be chilled, too. Frosty-cool vegetable soups that are blended smooth or left in tasty chunks are popular as appetizers or complete luncheons.

By teaming a meatless soup with a hearty bread containing cheese, eggs, milk, or whole grains, it becomes a substantial meal for the entire family.

New England Clam Chowder

2 tablespoons butter or margarine
½ cup finely diced celery
¼ cup thinly sliced leek (white part only)
¼ cup minced onion
¼ cup minced green pepper
3 tablespoons flour
1¾ cups milk
1 cup whipping cream or half-and-half
½ cup finely diced potato
12 large hard-shelled clams (to prepare, see Note), or 2 cans (about 7 ounces each) minced clams, drained (reserve liquid)
½ teaspoon salt
⅛ teaspoon thyme
3 drops Tabasco
Pinch white pepper
½ teaspoon Worcestershire sauce
Finely chopped parsley

1. Melt butter over low heat in a heavy 3-quart saucepan. Add celery, leek, onion, and green pepper. Stirring occasionally, cook 6 to 8 minutes, or until partially tender.
2. Blend flour into the vegetable-butter mixture; heat until bubbly. Gradually add milk and cream, stirring constantly. Bring to boiling, stirring constantly; cook 1 to 2 minutes.
3. Stir in potato, reserved clam liquid, salt, thyme, Tabasco, and pepper. Bring to boiling and simmer 25 to 35 minutes, stirring frequently. Add minced clams and Worcestershire sauce.
4. Pour into soup tureen or individual soup bowls. Garnish with parsley.

4 to 6 servings

Suggested accompaniment: Colonial Bread (page 20).

Note: To prepare clams and broth, rinse clams thoroughly under running cold water. Place clams in saucepan and add 3 cups water. Cook over medium heat until shells open completely. Drain the clams, reserving 2 cups of broth for chowder. Remove clams from shells. Cut off the hard outsides (combs) and chop clams into small, fine pieces. Decrease milk in chowder to 1 cup.

Creamy Tuna-Broccoli Soup

¼ cup butter or margarine
3 tablespoons minced onion
3 tablespoons flour
½ teaspoon salt
½ teaspoon celery salt
½ teaspoon ground sage
¼ teaspoon white pepper
Pinch cayenne pepper
1 quart milk
1 package (10 ounces) frozen chopped broccoli
1 can (6½ or 7 ounces) tuna, drained and flaked

1. Melt butter in a large, heavy saucepan over low heat. Add onion and cook until tender. Blend in flour, salt, celery salt, sage, and peppers. Heat until bubbly.
2. Gradually add milk, stirring constantly. Bring to boiling. Stir in broccoli. Cook over low heat, stirring occasionally, 10 to 12 minutes, or until broccoli is tender when pierced with a fork.
3. Mix in tuna and heat about 3 minutes.

About 6 servings

Suggested accompaniment: Family Wheat Bread (page 18).

Vegetable Oyster Soup

4 cups chopped head lettuce
2 cups chopped spinach
1 cup chopped carrots
½ cup chopped onion
1½ cups chicken broth or 1 can (about 10 ounces) chicken broth
1 can (10 ounces) frozen oysters, thawed
2 tablespoons butter
2 tablespoons flour
1¼ teaspoons salt
2 cups milk
1 teaspoon grated lemon peel
1 tablespoon lemon juice
Freshly ground pepper
Lemon slices

1. Put lettuce, spinach, carrots, onion, ½ cup chicken broth, and oysters into a 3-quart saucepan. Cover and cook until carrots are just tender (about 5 minutes).
2. Turn half of cooked mixture into an electric blender container and blend a few seconds; repeat. Set vegetable mixture aside.
3. Melt butter in a saucepan. Stir in flour and salt. Gradually add milk and remaining 1 cup chicken broth, stirring until smooth. Bring to boiling, stirring occasionally, and cook until thickened. Add vegetable mixture, lemon peel and juice, and pepper; heat to desired serving temperature, stirring occasionally.
4. Serve garnished with lemon slices.

About 7 cups

Suggested accompaniment: Crispy Breadsticks (page 55).

Cream of Broccoli Soup

2 packages (10 ounces each) frozen chopped broccoli
1 cup water
½ cup sliced celery
1 small onion, sliced
2 tablespoons butter or margarine
2 tablespoons flour
1½ quarts chicken stock
2 egg yolks, beaten
½ cup half-and-half or milk
½ teaspoon salt
Pinch pepper
Paprika

1. Cook broccoli in water 3 to 5 minutes; reserve liquid.
2. Sauté celery and onion in butter; stir in flour. Gradually add stock and liquid from broccoli, stirring constantly, until thickened.
3. Add broccoli; put through a food mill or purée in an electric blender, if desired.
4. Stir egg yolks into half-and-half; gradually add to soup, being careful not to boil. Season with salt and pepper.
5. Garnish each serving with a sprinkle of paprika.

6 servings

Suggested accompaniment: Cheddar Cornbread (page 42).

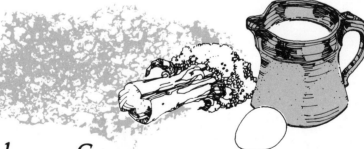

Chinese Cabbage Soup

2 cups cooked chicken, cut into strips (about 1 chicken breast)
7 cups chicken broth
6 cups sliced Chinese cabbage (celery cabbage)
1 teaspoon soy sauce
1 teaspoon salt
¼ teaspoon pepper

Combine chicken and chicken broth; bring to boiling. Stir in remaining ingredients; cook only 3 to 4 minutes, or just until cabbage is crisp-tender. (Do not overcook.)

6 servings

Note: If desired, lettuce may be substituted for the Chinese cabbage. Reduce cooking time to 1 minute.

Suggested accompaniment: Sesame Seed Twists (page 49).

Dill Cabbage Soup

Cook the vegetables only until crisp-tender to keep the flavor and appearance attractive.

2 quarts beef stock
1 cup thinly sliced carrots
1 cup sliced celery
½ cup chopped onion
8 cups (about ½ head) thinly sliced cabbage
Salt and pepper to taste
3 tablespoons water
2 tablespoons flour
½ cup yogurt or dairy sour half-and-half
½ teaspoon minced dill or ¼ teaspoon dried dill weed
Minced parsley

1. Pour stock into a large saucepan. Add carrots, celery, and onion. Bring to boiling, reduce heat, and cook until vegetables are tender (about 10 minutes).
2. Add cabbage; continue cooking until crisp-tender (about 5 minutes). Season to taste with salt and pepper.
3. Stir water gradually into flour, stirring until smooth. Pour slowly into soup, stirring constantly. Bring to boiling; boil 1 minute.
4. Stir in yogurt and dill.
5. Garnish with parsley.

8 to 10 servings

Suggested accompaniment: Refrigerator Rye Bread (page 18).

French Cauliflower Soup

1 head cauliflower, cut in flowerets
5 cups chicken stock or 5 chicken bouillon cubes in 5 cups water
½ cup uncooked rice
¼ cup finely chopped celery
1 cup milk or half-and-half
¼ cup flour
Salt and pepper
Sliced green onion, snipped watercress, or snipped parsley

1. Put cauliflowerets, stock, rice, and celery into a large saucepan. Bring to boiling; simmer until cauliflower is crisp-tender and rice is cooked (about 10 minutes).
2. Gradually add milk to flour, blending until smooth; stir into soup. Bring to boiling, stirring constantly until thickened. Season to taste.
3. Sprinkle each serving with green onion, watercress, or parsley.

6 servings

Suggested accompaniment: Dilly Cottage Batter Bread (page 25).

Creamed French Cauliflower Soup: Follow recipe for French Cauliflower Soup; strain soup after Step 1. Purée vegetables and rice in an electric blender. Return vegetables and stock to saucepot. Continue with Step 2. Stir in **¼ cup white wine** and either **½ teaspoon basil** or **¼ teaspoon dill weed.** Garnish as suggested.

Cream of Turkey Soup

½ cup butter
6 tablespoons flour
½ teaspoon salt
Pinch black pepper
2 cups half-and-half
3 cups turkey or chicken broth
¾ cup coarsely chopped cooked turkey

1. Heat butter in a saucepan. Blend in flour, salt, and pepper. Heat until bubbly.
2. Gradually add half-and-half and 1 cup of broth, stirring constantly. Bring to boiling; cook and stir 1 to 2 minutes.
3. Blend in remaining broth and turkey. Heat; do not boil. Garnish with grated carrot.

About 6 servings

Suggested accompaniment: Pleasin' Pumpkin Bread (page 42).

Frosty Cucumber Soup

1 large cucumber, scored with a
    fork
¼ teaspoon salt
    Pinch white pepper
1½ cups yogurt
1¼ cups water
½ cup walnuts, ground in an
    electric blender
2 cloves garlic, minced
    Green food coloring (optional)

1. Halve cucumber lengthwise and cut crosswise into very thin slices. Rub inside of a large bowl with cut surface of ½ clove garlic. Combine cucumber, salt, and pepper in bowl. Cover; chill.
2. Pour combined yogurt and water over chilled cucumber; mix well. If desired, tint with 1 or 2 drops of food coloring. Chill.
3. Combine walnuts and garlic; set aside for topping.
4. Ladle soup into bowls. Place soup bowls over larger bowls of crushed ice. Serve with walnut topping.

4 servings

Suggested accompaniment: Here's-to-Your-Health Bread (page 21).

Creamy Cheddar Cheese Soup

2 tablespoons butter
2 tablespoons chopped onion
⅓ cup all-purpose flour
1¼ teaspoons dry mustard
¼ teaspoon garlic powder
¼ teaspoon paprika
2 teaspoons Worcestershire sauce
1½ quarts milk
3 tablespoons chicken seasoned
    stock base
1½ cups sliced celery
2½ cups (10 ounces) shredded
    Cheddar cheese

1. Melt butter in a 3-quart saucepan. Add onion and sauté until tender. Stir in flour, mustard, garlic powder, paprika, and Worcestershire sauce.
2. Remove from heat; gradually add milk, stirring constantly. Add chicken stock base and celery; mix well. Cook over low heat, stirring occasionally, until thickened. Add cheese and stir until cheese is melted and soup is desired serving temperature; do not boil.
3. Serve topped with **chopped green pepper, pimento strips, toasted slivered almonds,** or **cooked crumbled bacon.**

About 2 quarts

Suggested accompaniment: Crispy Breadsticks (page 55).

Sweet Pea Soup

1 small head lettuce, shredded
    (about 5 cups)
2 cups shelled fresh peas, or 1
    package (10 ounces) frozen
    green peas
1 cup water
½ cup chopped leek or green onion
2 tablespoons butter
2 teaspoons chervil
1 teaspoon sugar
½ teaspoon salt
¼ teaspoon black pepper
1 can (about 10 ounces) condensed
    beef broth
¾ cup water
2 cups half-and-half

1. Put lettuce, peas, 1 cup water, leek, butter, chervil, sugar, salt, and pepper into a large saucepan; stir and bring to boiling. Cover and cook until peas are tender.
2. Press mixture through a coarse sieve or food mill and return to saucepan. Stir in broth and ¾ cup water.
3. Just before serving, stir half-and-half into mixture and heat.

6 servings

Suggested accompaniment: Cottage Raisin Puffs (page 37).

Pumpkin Patch Soup

If zipped in the blender before cooking, this soup becomes light and fluffy. You'll be left with an extra cup of pumpkin, so use it in Pumpkin Spice Rolls (page 28).

3 cups canned pumpkin or fresh cooked puréed pumpkin
2 cups milk, half-and-half, or 1 can (13 ounces) evaporated milk
3 tablespoons maple syrup
1 teaspoon salt
½ teaspoon nutmeg
½ teaspoon cinnamon
¼ teaspoon cloves or allspice

Combine all ingredients in a large saucepan. Heat.

4 servings

Suggested accompaniment: Cranberry Swirl Rolls (page 50).

Here are three variations of gazpacho, a Spanish soup with a refreshing flavor. All are naturals for fresh summer garden vegetables. Amounts of vegetables can vary according to what you have in your refrigerator, within reason.

Gazpacho

2 cans (6 ounces each) seasoned tomato juice
½ cucumber, coarsely sliced
1 tomato, quartered
¼ cup vinegar
¼ cup salad oil
1 tablespoon sugar
1 can or bottle (25.6 ounces) seasoned tomato juice
½ cucumber, chopped
1 tomato, chopped
1 small onion, chopped
Minced parsley
Chopped hard-cooked egg
Chopped cucumber
Croutons

1. Pour the 12 ounces tomato juice into an electric blender. Add sliced cucumber, tomato, vinegar, oil, and sugar; blend. Pour into a bowl and mix in remaining ingredients; chill.
2. Serve with bowls of parsley, hard-cooked egg, cucumber, and croutons.

4 servings

Tomato Cooler Gazpacho

2 cans (about 10 ounces each) condensed tomato soup
2 soup cans water
1 large clove garlic, crushed
1 tablespoon lemon juice
5 to 10 drops Tabasco
½ teaspoon crushed basil
½ cup chopped cucumber
½ cup chopped green pepper
2 tablespoons sliced green onion

1. Combine ingredients; chill several hours.
2. Serve in chilled sherbet glasses or bowls with garnishes suggested in Gazpacho.

6 servings

Gazpacho Garden Soup

3 large tomatoes, chopped
1 clove garlic, crushed
1 small cucumber, chopped
1 green pepper, chopped
½ cup sliced green onions
¼ cup chopped onion
¼ cup minced parsley
1 teaspoon crushed rosemary
¼ teaspoon crushed basil
½ teaspoon salt
¼ cup olive oil
¼ cup salad oil
2 tablespoons lemon juice
2 cups chicken broth or 3 chicken
  bouillon cubes dissolved in 2
  cups boiling water, then cooled

1. Combine all ingredients except chicken broth in a large bowl. Toss gently.
2. Stir in chicken broth; chill.
3. Serve in chilled bowls with garnishes suggested in Gazpacho.

6 servings

Pioneer Potato Soup

1 quart chicken stock
4 potatoes, chopped (about 4 cups)
2 cups sliced carrots
½ cup sliced celery
¼ cup chopped onion
1 teaspoon salt
½ teaspoon marjoram, dill weed, or
  cumin
⅛ teaspoon white pepper
1 cup milk or half-and-half
2 tablespoons flour
  Garnishes: paprika, sliced green
    onions, crisply cooked
    crumbled bacon, chopped
    pimento, snipped chives or
    parsley, or grated Parmesan
    cheese

1. Combine all ingredients except milk, flour, and garnishes in a large saucepan. Bring to boiling; simmer 30 minutes.
2. Gradually add milk to flour, stirring until smooth. Stir into soup.
3. Bring soup to boiling; boil 1 minute, stirring constantly.
4. Garnish as desired.

4 to 6 servings

Suggested accompaniment: Cheddar Cornbread (page 42).

Potato Soup with Sour Cream: Follow recipe for Pioneer Potato Soup. Before serving, stir in ½ **cup dairy sour cream.** Heat; do not boil.

Puréed Potato Soup: Follow recipe for either Pioneer Potato or Potato Soup with Sour Cream, omitting the flour. Purée in an electric blender before serving. Reheat, if necessary.

Lettuce Soup

Lettuce need not be relegated only to the salad bowl. Chop it up, stir it into a rich broth, and eat it with some San Francisco Sourdough French Bread (page 40).

2 tablespoons butter or margarine
2 tablespoons flour
1 can (about 10 ounces) condensed
  chicken broth
1 soup can water
½ small head lettuce, cored and
  coarsely chopped
¼ cup thinly sliced celery
1 tablespoon chopped watercress
  Salt and pepper

1. Melt butter in a saucepot; stir in flour and cook until bubbly.
2. Gradually stir in chicken broth and water; bring to boiling, stirring constantly. Cook 1 minute.
3. Stir in lettuce, celery, and watercress. Season with salt and pepper to taste. Cook until vegetables are crisp-tender, about 5 minutes.

About 3 servings

Mixed Vegetables Soup

3 cups beef broth or 3 beef
    bouillon cubes dissolved in 3
    cups boiling water
1 small potato, diced
2 carrots, diced
1 tomato, chopped
1 green onion, sliced
½ cup shredded cabbage or ½ cup
    sliced zucchini
½ teaspoon Beau Monde seasoning
    or seasoned salt
1 tablespoon minced parsley

1. Combine broth, potato, and carrot in a saucepan; bring to boiling. Simmer 30 minutes.
2. Add remaining ingredients; cook 5 minutes, or until cabbage is crisp-tender.

4 servings

Suggested accompaniment: Southern Buttermilk Biscuits (page 44).

SPECIAL OCCASION SOUPS

There is sure to come a time in your life when you'll want to serve something extra special for dinner. It may be a mother-in-law, an important client, the boss, or a best friend you want to impress with your culinary talents.

Whatever the reason, the soups in this section are truly elegant. You needn't tell your guests that these simply smashing soups are simple to make.

You may choose recipes for main dish soups like bouillabaisse, or delicate appetizer soups like consommé. Select breads which will harmonize with the soup entrée. The appetizer soups are not accompanied with bread suggestions since their main purpose is to stimulate the appetite.

Celery-Crab Soup

Quick, but elegant. Since it is so easy, you'll have time to make Popovers (page 48).

2 cans (about 10 ounces each)
    condensed cream of celery
    soup
2 soup cans milk
1 cup flaked crab meat
1 teaspoon Worcestershire sauce
¼ teaspoon crushed tarragon
4 to 8 drops Tabasco
    Butter (optional)
    Paprika (optional)

1. Combine soup and milk in a saucepot. Stir in crab meat, Worcestershire sauce, tarragon, and Tabasco. Heat (do not boil); stir occasionally.
2. Garnish each serving with a pat of butter and a sprinkling of paprika, if desired.

6 servings

Oyster Stew

If you like oysters, you'll love this—it's hardly more than oysters and milk. Traditionally, this is served Christmas Eve with buttered toast.

¼ cup butter or margarine
1 pint fresh oysters, drained;
   reserve liquor
1½ cups milk
1 cup half-and-half
1 teaspoon salt
   Pinch black pepper or cayenne
   pepper
   Minced parsley

1. Melt butter in a saucepan. Add milk, half-and-half, and oyster liquor. Scald; do not boil.
2. Add oysters and seasonings. Heat; do not boil.
3. Garnish with parsley.

4 servings

Lobster-Tomato Cream Soup

When you use lobster, you are really going first class. Serve with a bread equally as classy—French Crescents (page 28).

2 tablespoons minced onion
¼ cup butter
¼ cup flour
¼ teaspoon salt
   Pinch black pepper
2 cups tomato juice
1 cup half-and-half
½ cup milk
1½ teaspoons Worcestershire sauce
4 drops Tabasco
1 can (about 6 ounces) lobster,
   drained and cut in pieces
3 tablespoons dry sherry
   Whipped cream

1. Sauté onion in melted butter in a large saucepan. Stir in flour, salt, and pepper. Heat until mixture bubbles.
2. Gradually stir in tomato juice, half-and-half, milk, Worcestershire sauce, and Tabasco. Cook until sauce thickens, stirring constantly.
3. Add lobster, reserving a few pieces for garnish. Heat; do not boil. Stir in sherry.
4. Pour into a tureen or individual soup bowls. Garnish with reserved lobster meat and whipped cream.

6 servings

Crab-Tomato Cream Soup: Follow recipe for Lobster-Tomato Cream Soup, except substitute **1 cup** (about 4 ounces) **flaked fresh crab meat** for the lobster.

Creamy Shrimp and Avocado Bisque

Seafood and fruit join to make an elegant soup. Serve with bowknot-shaped Dinner Rolls (page 26).

2 cans (about 10 ounces each)
   condensed cream of asparagus
   soup
2 cans (about 10 ounces each)
   condensed cream of potato soup
1 teaspoon curry powder
2 soup cans milk
2 soup cans half-and-half
2 cups cooked shrimp, cut in pieces
   (see Note)
1 avocado, peeled and chopped
2 tablespoons minced chives

1. Combine soups and curry in a large, heavy saucepan. Stir in milk and half-and-half. Set over low heat until thoroughly heated, stirring occasionally.
2. Mix in shrimp; heat thoroughly; do not boil.
3. Pour into soup tureen; gently stir in avocado. Sprinkle with chives. Serve at once.

10 servings

Note: When using fresh or fresh-frozen shrimp, shell and devein. To remove the vein, make a shallow cut lengthwise down back of each shrimp. Remove vein with point of knife.

Cool and Creamy Shrimp and Avocado Bisque: Follow recipe for Creamy Shrimp and Avocado Bisque; chill before serving.

Bouillabaisse

Truly a bouillabaisse should be served after you've been fishing all day—so you can include your catch! But when you are buying, select 3 different fish plus seafood. Other possibilities besides those listed here are red snapper and whole clams.

⅔ cup chopped onion
2 leeks, chopped (white part only)
¼ cup olive oil
1 clove garlic, crushed
1 can (16 ounces) tomatoes
1 tablespoon minced parsley
½ bay leaf
½ teaspoon savory
½ teaspoon fennel
⅛ teaspoon saffron
1½ teaspoons salt
¼ teaspoon pepper
1 lobster (1½ to 2 pounds) cleaned
   and cut up, or 8 lobster tails
1½ pounds bass, boned and cut in
   1-inch pieces
1 pound perch, boned and cut in
   1-inch pieces
1 pound cod, boned and cut in
   1-inch pieces
1 pound fresh shelled deveined
   shrimp
1 pound sea scallops (fresh or
   thawed frozen)
1 pint oysters
6 slices French bread, toasted

1. Sauté onion and leeks in olive oil in a large Dutch oven. Stir in garlic, tomatoes, parsley, bay leaf, savory, fennel, saffron, salt, pepper, lobster, and bass, and just enough water to cover (1 to 1½ quarts). Bring to boiling; simmer 10 minutes.
2. Add perch and cod; continue to simmer 10 minutes, or until fish are almost tender.
3. Add shrimp and scallops; cook 5 minutes longer.
4. Meanwhile, drain oysters, reserving liquor. Remove any shell particles. Simmer oysters in liquor in a saucepan 3 minutes, or until edges begin to curl. Add to fish mixture.
5. Line a deep serving dish with toasted bread. Cover with fish and pour sauce in which fish has been cooked over all. Serve at once.

About 8 servings

Note: If desired, substitute 1 cup sherry for 1 cup of the water in step 1.

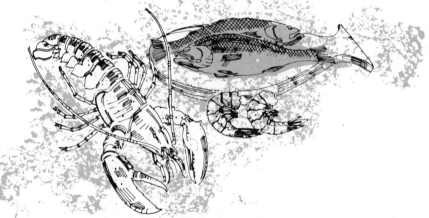

Consommé

More than just a clear stock, consommé derives its special flavor from the vegetables used. Egg whites and shells clarify this traditional and elegant appetizer soup.

½ cup coarsely chopped celery
   leaves
½ cup chopped leek (green part
   only)
½ cup chopped carrots
¼ cup chopped parsley leaves and
   stems
2 tomatoes, chopped
3 egg whites
3 egg shells, crushed
2 quarts beef stock

1. Combine ingredients in a heavy 4- or 5-quart saucepot. Bring to boiling. Reduce heat; simmer 20 minutes, uncovered and undisturbed.
2. Pour soup into a sieve lined with a double thickness of dampened cheesecloth which has been placed over a large bowl. Serve hot.

6 servings

Double Consommé: Follow recipe for Consommé, adding **1 pound beef,** cut in pieces, with vegetables. Simmer 45 minutes.

Consommé with Vegetables: Follow recipe for Consommé. After straining, add **1 cup thinly sliced cooked vegetables.** Heat.

Vegetable Medley Soup, 70

Vichyssoise *(Chilled Leek and Potato Soup)*

Surprisingly enough, this is an American soup with a French name. Gourmets will insist that it be made with the white part of leeks. (The rest of us will settle for green onions.) Serve very cold.

4 to 6 leeks
2 tablespoons butter or margarine
4 potatoes, pared and sliced
1 quart chicken broth or 6 chicken bouillon cubes dissolved in 1 quart boiling water
1 cup half-and-half
1 cup chilled whipping cream
Snipped chives

1. Finely slice the white part and about an inch of the green part of each leek to measure about 1 cup.
2. Sauté leeks in butter in a heavy saucepan. Stir in potatoes and broth; bring to boiling. Simmer 40 minutes, or until potatoes are tender.
3. Sieve the cooked vegetables or blend until smooth in an electric blender. Mix in half-and-half; chill thoroughly.
4. Just before serving, stir in whipping cream. Garnish with chives.

8 servings

Sour Cream Garlic Soup

Garlic lovers—this one would be a nice beginning to a pork entrée.

8 cloves garlic, crushed or minced
⅓ cup butter or margarine
⅓ cup flour
¼ teaspoon crushed basil
⅛ teaspoon salt
⅛ teaspoon pepper
1½ quarts beef broth
Dairy sour cream
Chopped chives
Sieved hard-cooked egg yolk

1. Carefully cook garlic in melted butter in a heavy saucepan until golden, stirring constantly. Stir in flour, basil, salt, and pepper; heat until bubbly. Gradually add broth, stirring constantly. Bring to boiling; cook 1 minute.
2. Serve hot or cold, topping each serving with a generous dollop of sour cream and a sprinkling of chives and egg yolk.

4 to 6 servings

New Orleans Gumbo

Gumbo, a Creole masterpiece, is traditionally made with filé, which is dried sassafras leaves. Because filé is not always available outside of Louisiana, okra is often substituted for it.

2 onions, chopped
½ cup butter or margarine
¼ cup flour
2 quarts chicken stock
1 can (28 ounces) tomatoes
½ pound okra, sliced
1 stalk celery, sliced
½ teaspoon thyme
1 bay leaf
½ teaspoon salt
Pinch pepper
Pinch cayenne pepper
6 hard-shell crabs
24 large peeled and deveined shrimp
24 oysters
2 cups cooked rice

1. Sauté onion in butter in a large saucepan. Mix in flour; cook until bubbly.
2. Gradually add chicken stock, tomatoes, okra, celery, and seasonings; add crabs. Simmer 1 hour.
3. Add shrimp and oysters; simmer 5 minutes.
4. Put ¼ cup rice into each soup bowl; ladle in hot gumbo.

8 servings

Crab Meat Bisque

Bisques are cream soups usually containing shellfish, as here. Accompany any one of these bisques with crescent-shaped Dinner Rolls (page 26).

½ cup chopped onion
⅓ cup chopped carrot
1 leek (white part only), minced
3 tablespoons butter or margarine
1 quart White Stock (see page 62)
1 teaspoon salt
⅛ teaspoon pepper
1 bay leaf
3 egg yolks, beaten
1 cup whipping cream
½ cup dry white wine
2 cups (8 ounces) flaked fresh crab meat
   Minced parsley

1. Sauté onion, carrot, and leek in melted butter in a large saucepan. Stir in white stock, salt, pepper, and bay leaf. Cover; simmer 10 minutes.
2. Push mixture through sieve or food mill or purée in an electric blender. Return to saucepan.
3. Stir about 3 tablespoons hot soup into egg yolks. Return mixture to soup, stirring constantly.
4. Stir in whipping cream, wine, and crab meat. Heat; do not boil.
5. Sprinkle parsley over each serving.

8 servings

Lobster Bisque: Follow recipe for Crab Meat Bisque, substituting **2 cans (about 6 ounces each) lobster meat,** drained, for the crab meat.

Shrimp Bisque: Follow recipe for Crab Meat Bisque, substituting **2½ cups chopped cooked shrimp** for crab meat.

Toasted Almond Soup

This creamy soup is not only delicious but quick, because it is made in an electric blender.

1 cup water
1 cup salted roasted almonds
4 egg yolks
3 chicken bouillon cubes
1 small slice onion
½ teaspoon sugar
2 cups water
1 cup half-and-half

1. Put 1 cup water, almonds, egg yolks, bouillon cubes, onion, and sugar in an electric blender container. Blend until amonds are finely ground.
2. Pour into a saucepan; stir in 2 cups water. Cook over low heat about 5 minutes, or until mixture coats a spoon, stirring constantly (do not boil).
3. Stir in half-and-half and heat thoroughly without boiling. Garnish with **finely shredded orange peel.**

5 or 6 servings

BREAKFAST SOUPS

Soup for breakfast? Why not? What could be nicer than a refreshing bowl of chilled fruit or eggnog soup to start the day?

These recipes show you how easy it is to treat everyday foods a little differently to make delicious breakfast soup combinations.

Sometimes even the cook needs a bright wake-me-up in the morning. Treat yourself and the rest of the early birds with a light fruit soup. If you aren't the type to be well organized in the morning, you can prepare the fruits the night before to be thoroughly chilled and waiting to get all of you off to a fresh start the next morning.

Teaming the soup with whole grain or enriched breads and/or a meat or cheese, it is possible to serve a nutritious breakfast to each individual as he appears and then dashes off to go his own way.

Crimson Soup

4 cups puréed drained tomatoes
   (about 2 pounds ripe tomatoes)
1 tablespoon brown sugar
1 teaspoon salt
  Few grains freshly ground black
   pepper
½ teaspoon grated lemon peel
2 tablespoons lemon juice
½ teaspoon grated onion
1 cup finely chopped cantaloupe
½ cup finely chopped honeydew
   melon
¼ cup finely chopped cucumber

1. Combine tomato purée, brown sugar, salt, pepper, lemon peel and juice, and onion. Stir in remaining ingredients.
2. Chill several hours.
3. Serve in chilled bowls. If desired, garnish each serving with a lemon slice and a sprig of parsley or watercress. Accompany with a shaker of seasoned salt and a bowl of brown sugar.

6 servings

Sour Cream Cherry Soup

1 quart water
2 to 2½ pounds frozen sweetened
   tart red cherries, slightly
   thawed
½ teaspoon salt
½ cup cold water
¼ cup flour
3 egg yolks, slightly beaten
1 cup dairy sour cream

1. Bring the water to boiling in a large saucepan. Add cherries and salt; bring to boiling; simmer, covered, 10 minutes.
2. Pour the cold water into a 1-pint screw-top jar. Add flour; cover jar tightly; shake until blended.
3. Stirring constantly, slowly pour flour mixture into hot cherry mixture; bring to boiling, and cook 2 to 3 minutes.
4. Remove from heat; gradually add ⅓ cup hot soup to the egg yolks, stirring vigorously; blend into soup. Stirring constantly, cook over low heat 3 to 5 minutes (do not boil). Remove from heat.
5. Gradually add 1 cup hot soup to the sour cream, stirring vigorously; then blend into remaining soup. Chill and serve cold, or serve hot, if desired.

8 to 10 servings

Swedish Fruit Soup

1 cup dried apricots
¾ cup dried apples
½ cup dried peaches
½ cup prunes
½ cup dark seedless raisins
2 quarts water
¼ cup sugar
3 tablespoons quick-cooking
   tapioca
1 piece stick cinnamon (3 inches)
1 teaspoon grated orange peel
1 cup red raspberry fruit syrup

1. Rinse dried fruits with cold water; remove pits from prunes. Place fruits in a large kettle with the water; cover and allow to soak 2 to 3 hours.
2. Add the sugar, tapioca, cinnamon, and orange peel to fruits; let stand 5 minutes. Bring to boiling and simmer covered 1 hour, or until fruit is tender.
3. Stir in syrup; cool, then chill thoroughly.
4. Serve with **whipped cream** and **slivered blanched almonds**.

12 to 16 servings

Breakfast Nog

¼ cup sugar
2 egg yolks
1 quart milk
¼ teaspoon salt
⅛ teaspoon nutmeg
1 teaspoon vanilla extract

1. Beat sugar into egg yolks in a large saucepan. Stir in milk, salt, and nutmeg. Cook over low heat, stirring constantly, until mixture coats a spoon.
2. Serve hot or cold in mugs.

4 servings

Banana Nog: Prepare Breakfast Nog. Chill. Stir in **1 or 2 sliced bananas.** If desired, sprinkle each serving with **grated chocolate** and **cinnamon.**

Fluffy Breakfast Nog: Prepare Breakfast Nog; chill. Beat **2 egg whites** until foamy. Gradually add **3 tablespoons sugar,** beating until soft peaks form. Fold into chilled custard. Top each serving with dollop of **whipped cream.**

Cherry Breakfast Soup

1 can (about 10 ounces) dark sweet
    cherries, drained; reserve liquid
4 whole cloves
1 stick cinnamon, broken in half
    Juice of ½ lemon (about 2
    tablespoons)
2 teaspoons cornstarch
1 can (16 ounces) sliced pears,
    drained; reserve juice
1 orange, peeled and sectioned

1. Combine cherry liquid, cloves, cinnamon, and lemon juice in a saucepan; bring to boiling. Simmer 5 minutes. Remove spices with slotted spoon.
2. Combine cornstarch and pear juice; gradually add to cherry mixture. Cook until thickened, stirring constantly.
3. Stir in remaining fruit. Serve hot or cold.

6 servings

Apricot-Melon Soup

2 cups chopped melon, cantaloupe,
    or honeydew
2 cups apricot nectar
2 tablespoons lemon juice
    Dash salt
1 pint lemon sherbet

1. Combine melon, apricot nectar, lemon juice, and salt. Chill.
2. Serve in chilled bowls. Float a scoop of sherbet on each serving.

4 servings

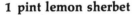

SHORT-CUT SOUPS

Cooking creatively with convenience is the secret of serving quick, tasty meals. You can dress up a basic canned soup by adding seasonings, vegetables, meats . . . just about anything you like.

Included in this section are some delicious ideas for those hurry-up days when dinner has to be on the table in 15 minutes, or when you just don't feel like spending a lot of time in the kitchen.

Here are some suggestions of how to beat the clock with soups:

1. Prepare and freeze some soup stocks. Check page 62 for preparation methods. Don't forget to label the freezer container with the name and date for easy reference later.

2. Make a double batch of soup and freeze the extra for a treat later.

3. When you are making a soup-accompaniment bread recipe that makes two or more loaves, get into the habit of tucking one away in the freezer for emergencies.

4. Keep extra cans of soup on hand so you can add your own special touches for easy meals.

Green Pea Potage

Water chestnuts are a unique soup ingredient, for no matter how long they sit in the soup, they never get soggy and lose their crunch.

¼ cup dairy sour cream
1 can (about 11 ounces) condensed
    green pea soup
1 soup can water
¼ cup sliced water chestnuts
1 tablespoon sliced green onion
1 tablespoon lemon juice
    Toasted slivered almonds

1. Blend sour cream into soup in a bowl. Gradually add water, stirring until smooth. Mix in water chestnuts, green onion, and lemon juice. Chill 4 hours.
2. Garnish chilled soup with the almonds.

3 servings

Suggested accompaniment: Sesame Seed Twists (page 49).

Tomato-Noodle Soup

Tomatoes and noodles join to make this reminiscent of spaghetti!

2 cans (about 10 ounces each)
    condensed tomato soup
2 cans (about 10 ounces each)
    condensed cream of celery
    soup
1 can (6 ounces) tomato paste
¼ cup instant minced onion
1 can (1 ounce) dried instant mixed
    vegetables
1 teaspoon salt
¼ teaspoon pepper
1 teaspoon crushed basil
2 quarts water
8 ounces (about 4 cups) fine egg
    noodles
    Milk

1. Combine soups and tomato paste in a large saucepan; mix in instant minced onion, instant vegetables, salt, pepper, and basil.
2. Gradually add water, stirring constantly. Bring to boiling, stirring occasionally.
3. Add noodles gradually so the mixture continues to boil. Cook, uncovered, until noodles are tender, about 10 minutes, stirring occasionally. Blend in milk to taste.

About 3½ quarts

Suggested accompaniment: Garlic Bread (page 50).

Creamy Shrimp Gumbo

Shrimp makes it elegant, canned soups make it quick.

1 can (about 10 ounces) condensed
   cream of chicken soup
1 soup can milk
1 can (about 10 ounces) condensed
   chicken gumbo soup
½ cup chopped cooked shrimp
¼ teaspoon soy sauce
   Garlic powder to taste

1. Blend chicken soup and milk in a saucepan.
2. Stir in remaining ingredients. Heat (do not boil).

4 to 6 servings

Suggested accompaniment: Warmed mini-loaf of Basic White Bread (page 14).

Chilled Dilled Chicken Soup

2 cans (about 10 ounces each)
   condensed cream of chicken
   soup
2 soup cans milk
2 teaspoons chopped green onion
   with tops
½ cup chopped cucumber
2 teaspoons chopped fresh dill or
   ½ teaspoon dill weed

1. Mix soup and milk in a bowl; blend in the remaining ingredients.
2. Cover and refrigerate 3 to 4 hours to allow flavors to blend.
3. Serve soup thoroughly chilled, or heat and serve.

About 6 servings

Suggested accompaniment: Rhubarb Bread (page 43).

Cream of Everything Soup

Mushroom, peas, tomato, rice are all blended to perfection.

1 can (about 10 ounces) condensed
   cream of mushroom soup
1 can (about 11 ounces) condensed
   green pea soup
1 can (about 10 ounces) condensed
   tomato-rice soup
3 soup cans water
½ teaspoon crushed dill weed
¼ teaspoon crushed tarragon
   Dairy sour cream

1. Combine all ingredients in a saucepan. Cover and simmer about 10 minutes.
2. Top individual bowls of soup with a dollop of dairy sour cream.

About 8 servings

Suggested accompaniment: Oklahoma Oatmeal Bread (page 44).

Herbed Soup

Two herbs here you should get to know. Basil complements most tomato dishes, while fennel, a mild licorice flavor, enhances the taste of fish.

1 can (about 10 ounces) condensed
    chicken gumbo soup
1 can (about 10 ounces) condensed
    cream of celery soup
2 soup cans water
¼ teaspoon ground fennel
¼ teaspoon crushed basil
    Few grains ground ginger
    Avocado Sauce

1. Blend soups, water, herbs, and ginger in a saucepan. Simmer covered about 10 minutes.
2. Serve with Avocado Sauce.

6 servings

Suggested accompaniment: Sunshine Cornbread (page 46).

Avocado Sauce: Combine **½ cup dairy sour cream** and **½ cup mashed ripe avocado;** blend until smooth.

Canyon City Soup

Seasonings in this soup give it a southwestern flavor.

1 onion, sliced
2 tablespoons margarine
½ pound frankfurters, sliced
3½ cups (28 ounces) tomatoes
2 cups (about 15 ounces) kidney
    beans or chili beans, drained
½ to 1 teaspoon chili powder
½ teaspoon cumin powder
½ teaspoon garlic salt
    Salt and pepper

1. Sauté onion in margarine.
2. Add remaining ingredients; stir.
3. Simmer 10 minutes.

4 servings

Suggested accompaniment: Sunshine Cornbread (page 46).

Curried Potato-Apple Soup

1 can (about 10 ounces) condensed
    cream of potato soup
1 soup can milk
1 apple, quartered, pared, and
    cored
½ teaspoon curry powder

1. Combine all ingredients in electric blender container and blend until smooth.
2. Pour into a saucepan and heat thoroughly.
3. Garnish hot soup with **apple wedges.**

About 1 quart

Suggested accompaniment: Cinnamon Swirl Date Ring (page 51).

Zucchini Soup

Zucchini grows so abundantly and quickly that it is a fun vegetable to watch in the garden.

2 cups diced zucchini
½ cup tomato juice
2 tablespoons chopped onion
⅛ teaspoon basil
1 package (8 ounces) cream cheese, cubed

1. Combine zucchini, tomato juice, onion, and basil; simmer 20 minutes.
2. Pour into an electric blender; add cream cheese and blend until smooth.
3. Serve hot, or chill to serve as cold soup or dip.

About 3 servings

Suggested accompaniment: La Verde Slices (page 50).

Vegetable-Sausage Soup

1 can (about 10 ounces) condensed vegetable soup
1 soup can water
½ teaspoon prepared mustard
⅛ teaspoon pepper
1 cup cubed thuringer or cervelat sausage

1. Combine soup, water, mustard, and pepper in a saucepan. Set over moderate heat until mixture begins to simmer.
2. Add the sausage and simmer 10 minutes.

3 servings

Suggested accompaniment: Delicatessen Rye Bread (page 17).

Caraway Bouillon

1½ quarts boiling water
6 beef bouillon cubes
1 tablespoon crushed caraway seed

1. Add water to bouillon and caraway seed in a saucepan. Stir until cubes are dissolved. Cover; simmer 10 minutes.
2. Serve hot in mugs.

6 to 8 servings

Suggested accompaniment: Peasant Black Bread (page 56).

Vegetable Bouillon

1 can (about 10 ounces) condensed beef broth
1 soup can water
1 can (6 ounces) cocktail vegetable juice
2 tablespoons finely chopped green pepper
3 radishes, finely chopped
½ teaspoon instant minced onion

1. Bring broth, water, and vegetable juice to boiling in a saucepan.
2. Add green pepper, radishes, and onion. Simmer, uncovered, 5 to 8 minutes.
3. Serve hot, garnished with sprigs of **parsley**.

4 servings

Suggested accompaniment: Zucchini Bread (page 43).

California Cup

Although the ingredients sound unusual, the combination is surprisingly good.

1 can (about 10 ounces) condensed
    tomato soup
½ soup can cranberry juice cocktail
½ soup can water
1 teaspoon lemon juice
    Dairy sour cream

1. Combine ingredients; chill until serving time.
2. Top each serving with dollop of sour cream.

3 servings

Suggested accompaniment: toasted Here's-to-Your-Health Bread (page 21).

Cabbage-Cheese Chowder

The brisk autumn air and activities are sure to stimulate appetites.

1 can (about 10 ounces) condensed
    Cheddar cheese soup
1 soup can milk
½ teaspoon prepared mustard
4 slices (2 ounces) bologna, diced
3 cups thinly sliced cabbage

1. Combine soup, milk, and mustard in a medium saucepan. Stir in bologna and cabbage.
2. Cook over low heat until cabbage is crisp-tender, about 5 minutes.

4 servings

Suggested accompaniment: Carrot Brown Bread (page 19).

Quick Mulligatawny

Creamy curried chicken soup is a quick adaptation of a well-known Indian soup.

1 can (about 10 ounces) condensed
    cream of chicken soup
1 soup can milk
1 cup finely chopped cooked
    chicken
¼ cup packaged precooked rice
½ teaspoon curry powder
¼ teaspoon instant minced onion

1. Combine all ingredients in a medium saucepan.
2. Simmer 10 minutes.

4 servings

Suggested accompaniment: Ground Nut Bread (page 22).

Egg Drop Soup

Oriental in origin, Egg Drop Soup is an appetizing first course.

¼ cup thinly sliced celery
2 tablespoons thinly sliced
   mushrooms
1 green onion, thinly sliced
3 cups chicken stock
½ teaspoon salt
   Few grains pepper
1 egg, well beaten

1. Combine vegetables and chicken stock in a saucepan. Stir in salt and pepper. Bring to boiling; simmer 5 minutes.
2. Reduce heat and drizzle egg slowly into stock while stirring. Stir until egg separates into shreds. Simmer 1 minute. Serve at once.

3 or 4 servings

Suggested accompaniment: Drop Biscuits (page 45).

Herbed Zucchini Soup

½ cup chopped onion
2 tablespoons bacon fat or
   margarine
4 medium zucchini, sliced (about 4
   cups)
1 can (about 10 ounces) condensed
   beef consommé or broth
2 cups water
1 teaspoon basil
½ teaspoon salt
¼ teaspoon garlic powder
⅛ teaspoon pepper
¼ cup minced parsley or 2
   tablespoons dried parsley
   Grated Parmesan cheese

1. Sauté onion in bacon fat in a large saucepan. Stir in remaining ingredients except Parmesan cheese. Heat to boiling; simmer until zucchini is tender, 3 to 5 minutes.
2. Sprinkle each serving with Parmesan cheese.

4 to 6 servings

Suggested accompaniment: Homemade Croutons (page 49).

Creamy Zucchini Soup without Cream:
Prepare Herbed Zucchini Soup. Purée in an electric blender. Reheat.

ADVENTURES IN BREAD SCULPTURE

The art of sculpting wonderful things out of bread dough has caught the imaginations of adults and children alike.

The fascinating part is that the dough is pliable enough for all stages of interest and development. It is great for children to play with on rainy days to work off that excess energy . . . and even have something to show for it. It can be a learning tool for teaching shapes, the alphabet, numbers, animals, etc.

Bread dough can also be made into decorative items for the house, for gifts, for Christmas ornaments, containers—the list is limited only by one's creativity.

You can do anything with it except eat it.

It is a fun indoor sport—and inexpensive. All the tools and ingredients you will need are already in your home.

TOOLS FOR BREAD SCULPTURE

Common household items give a variety of shapes and textures to your creations. Here is a partial list of tools to help you design in dough:

—cookie cutters

—knives, forks, spoons

—garlic press

—colander

—scissors

—brushes

—nails

—cake, candy, or gelatin molds

—melon-ball cutters

—wooden picks

—tops of aerosol cans

BASIC DOUGH

Combine 2 cups all-purpose flour and 1 cup salt in a large mixing bowl. Gradually add 1 cup water, stirring constantly until mixture forms a ball. (The amount of water needed may vary depending on the humidity in the air. Be careful not to add too much water so dough becomes sticky.) Knead on lightly floured board until smooth and firm (about 8 to 10 minutes). Place dough in a plastic bag to prevent drying out.

HINTS FOR PERFECT DOUGH

Always flour your hands and work surfaces to prevent sticking.

Don't use self-rising flour because the leavening in the flour will cause the sculpture to puff out of shape.

The dough may be stored in a plastic bag in the refrigerator up to 5 days.

If dough becomes dry, pat on a little more water and knead until it returns to its proper consistency. If dough becomes too sticky, knead in additional flour.

Wipe oil on gelatin or cake molds before pressing in the dough for easier removal and cleaner impression.

Food coloring may be added at different times to give different effects. For a uniform color, add food coloring to the water. For a marbled effect, add it while kneading the dough.

HARDENING PROCESSES

There are two basic ways to make your sculpture permanent. Either air drying or oven baking will make it hard for the finishing touches.

Air Drying. Although it takes longer, it is easier for kids to do themselves. It also produces interesting textures. Place sculpture on a screen or wire rack so that the air can equally reach both sides. Allow it to dry at least 48 hours until it is completely hard and is white in appearance.

Oven Drying. Place sculpture on foil-covered baking sheets. Bake at 325° to 350°F until it is a light, golden brown. Allow 30 minutes for each ¼ inch of thickness.

HINTS FOR BAKING

Bake as soon after shaping as possible to avoid crumbling.

If bubbling or puffing occurs, prick with a pin or wooden pick and reduce baking temperature by 50° to 75°.

Cracks can be corrected by filling in with moistened dough and allowing to dry.

Thinner pieces of sculpture will dry faster. To avoid burning, watch carefully and if necessary lower the oven temperature.

If the sculpture has a tendency to curl during baking, hold down the edges with a heavy object or metal tool. (You might raid the workshop for suitable objects.) Place these on the dough shapes after they have begun to harden. (Test hardness with a spoon; this will insure not leaving an unwanted impression on the dough.)

FINISHING TECHNIQUES

To give your sculpture that enduring, polished look, there are several finishes that may be applied. Many of the finishes add decorative as well as sealer properties to preserve the sculpture. Sealing is necessary to protect it from humidity and moisture and makes it washable. Any color under the rainbow is at your fingertips to individualize your art.

The simplest finish is to shellac, varnish, or coat with lacquer or acrylic clear gloss sealer. Both sides must be brushed evenly to insure complete protection.

Egg or Milk Finish. Brush the sculpture with a thin coat of egg yolk or egg white or whole beaten egg or milk. For lighter browning, allow sculpture to bake about 15 minutes, then brush with egg and return to oven. For darker browning, continue to brush every 10 or 15 minutes during baking.

Watercolor Finish. Paint the sculpture with any watercolor you choose, then varnish.

Acrylic Paint Finish. Paint with acrylic paints to seal the sculpture. This makes varnishing and other final sealing agents unnecessary.

Antique Finish. Apply two coats of acrylic lacquer to sculpture, then one coat of commercial wood stain. Allow to dry a few minutes, then rub surface with a soft cloth to give a highlighted effect. Seal with a coat of varnish.

Metallic Finish. Paint sculpture dark metallic green, then apply a rub-on metallic finish (copper, gold, silver, or bronze) to highlight. Seal with a coat of varnish.

Special Effects. Sprinkle or glue onto the wet finish one of the following: sequins, small pieces of pasta, buttons, rhinestones, seeds, beads, bells, or other decorations.

ORNAMENTS AND GIFTS

Here is your chance to create a kaleidoscope of shapes for decoration, for use, or just for fun.

CHRISTMAS ORNAMENTS

Hanging cookie-cutter shapes on the tree can really add a warm, homey touch to the holidays. It is also a project that can be enjoyed by the whole family.

For shapes like candy canes or wreaths, just twist or braid three ropes of dough together. Then turn into a cane or wreath shape. Remember to color them red and white or green when adding the water to the dough. Berries, little round balls of dough, or leaves cut out with cookie cutters and the veins drawn in with a wooden pick, can dress up the wreath easily.

Other free-form shapes like animals, angels, and faces are also simple to do.

To hang, pull a piece of string or colored twine through a hole in the top to hook on the branch.

To form a candle holder, make thick ropes of dough and twist together. Form three wreaths around the candle for size, one on top of another. Glue together with water. Make a bow and attach by moistening with water. Remove the candle. Bake, cool, color, and varnish. For variation, place leaves, elves, or other forms around the bottom before baking.

To form tree ornaments:

1. Roll out dough on lightly floured surface to ¼-inch thickness.

2. With cookie cutter, cut out desired shapes and place on foil-covered baking sheet.

3. Eyes, nose, cheeks, buttons, and other decorations can be added by rolling small pieces of dough between your fingers until they form a small ball. Then moisten with water and place on the sculpture.

4. Hair, beards, tails, etc., can be made by pressing dough through a garlic press or colander, or rolling long pieces of dough to the thickness of spaghetti.

5. With a nail, make indentations for eyes, buttons, etc., and a hole for hanging by a string.

6. Bake at 325° to 350°F until light brown. Cool on wire rack or screen; varnish.

GIFTS

Bread sculpture makes a thoughtful, inexpensive gift because you designed and made it yourself. Jewelry, bread baskets, mirror and picture frames, and door initials are all in demand. Enjoy the fun of making and giving these unique pieces of art.

Mirror Frames. Cut shape of mirror out of foil. Place on foil-lined baking sheet. Arrange cut-out shapes on top of the mirror-shaped foil on a baking sheet. Glue the pieces together with water. Bake, cool, color, and varnish. Glue with white glue onto mirror.

Variation. Roll out dough. Cut into 2- to 3-inch-wide rectangular strips. Cut to fit around a piece of foil the same shape as mirror or picture on baking sheet. Etch designs on top. Glue together with water at the joints. Bake, cool, color, and varnish.

Picture Frames. Cut a piece of foil the size of the picture. Form the dough around the sample, right on the foil-covered baking sheet. Cut-out designs or rolled strips of decorated dough are attractive. Bake, cool, and finish as desired. Place picture on heavy cardboard. Cover outside rims with baked dough sculpture. Secure with glue.

Name Plaques. With a long, thin rope of dough write the name of a person and bake. Glue onto finished wood pieces and nail on the bedroom door or wherever desired.

Kids' Plaques. Animals, letters, or story-book characters may either be glued directly to the wall or on colored pieces of wood for an exciting children's wall. Alphabet letters and numbers are fun to make and are great teaching tools.

Jewelry or Macramé Beads. Since the natural look is in vogue, making your own jewelry is not only inexpensive but smart looking. Unique-looking beads can be large or small and are suitable for stringing or weaving into macramé designs. To make jewelry beads:

1. Shape small pieces of dough into balls. For round beads, simply leave as balls. For variations, flatten, make oval, square, or oblong.

2. With a skewer or nail, make a hole in center of each bead for stringing.

3. After drying or baking on foil-lined baking sheets, paint with watercolors or acrylic paints, if desired. When dry, varnish to seal. You may find spray varnish helpful for sealing such small objects.

Woven Baskets and Pots. To make baskets and pots:

1. Roll out dough on lightly floured surface to ⅜- to ½-inch thickness. Cut into 1-inch-wide strips.

2. Weave these strips on a piece of foil.

3. Grease outside of a 9×5×3-inch loaf pan or round casserole or clay pot and place upside-down on baking sheet. Press woven dough strips gently over pan.

4. Bake at 325° to 350°F until partially firm. Remove from oven. Turn right-side up.

5. Moisten a braided or twisted strip of dough and press onto rim of basket. Flowers or other cut designs may be added. Continue to bake until completely hardened. Cool. Coat with the finish of your choice.

INDEX